Dick Jo
of the
Hoylake Horse

This book is dedicated to the memory of Dick and Joan Jones

by
Mike Priestley

Published in the United Kingdom by

Michael G. Priestley Books
19, Ridgeway Close,
Farnsfield, Newark,
Nottinghamshire.
NG22 8DT.
michaelgpriestley@live.co.uk

A CIP record of this book is available from the British Library.

First printed 2014.

Cover design by Kate Shea.

Layout and design by Unwin Print

ISBN 978 0 9574134 3 6

Other books by Michael G Priestley

Merseyside in Monochrome
Train Spotters
Double Arrow Double Royal
The Priestley Collection, Scenes from a Victorian Photograph Album
Youth Hostellers
Diesels

Dick Jones
of the
Hoylake Horse

Contents   Page

1. Introduction

Christine Jones and I were relaxing on the long grey settee that could operate as a bed when required. It had a flat leather effect seat and a matching fabric back and it was placed directly opposite to the fireplace and the TV. Running the length of the house, the sitting room was well lit with windows at both ends. The tea time news had just started when the front door opened and then closed again and I picked myself up and sat forward, with just a degree of apprehension.

Dick Jones put his head round the door to the lounge, enquiringly. "Hi Dad, this is Mike," Chris announced. He gave me a quick glance, with maybe not so much a smile as a knowing grin, or so I decided. "Hello, Mike," he replied, giving little else away, before disappearing towards the kitchen.

It was the spring of 1967 and it was the first time I had visited 76, School Lane. Chris had finished her late afternoon newspaper round, delivering the Liverpool Echo in her own neighbourhood of Wallasey Village. Having accompanied her home, I had already been introduced to her mum, Joan, busily preparing the evening meal for the usual seven occupants. That included Chris's grandma, who had come to live with them because of her failing health, her two older brothers, David and Malcolm and her sister Jenny, who was also David's twin.

I thought her dad might be a little suspicious to find that Chris's new friend was in the same school year as his elder son Malcolm and therefore four years older than his younger daughter, but if he knew this he showed no concern. Perhaps I just did not look my age. I had my prepared explanation ready. Our group of male friends were seeing various members of Chris's school friendship group. It wasn't just me that was a "cradle snatcher."

The explanation I had decided on in my head lay unused and indeed was never called upon. I was not put on the spot then or thereafter. In the years that followed, Dick Jones never made me account for myself, though there were occasions when I might have given him reason to feel tempted. It would not have been shyness or a reluctance to speak his mind that would have stopped him giving me a bit of a quizzing. Dick Jones had an outgoing personality.

This tea time scenario was to be repeated many times over in the following weeks and months, stretching eventually to years, but Dick's arrival home from work was not always quite such a placid affair. Dick worked for R.O. Edwards and Company, a timber merchant in Liverpool, as a salesman of hardwood timber. This took him all over Lancashire, initially by bus or train and with a lot of leg work thrown in as well. By the time I got to know him, he had the assistance of a company car.

Later on, a company take-over meant that his patch grew considerably, to include Yorkshire and other parts of the North of England. Sometimes he would be required to stay away from Wallasey overnight and frequently the long hours on pre-motorway roads meant he was late getting back home again.

It struck me early on, no doubt reinforced by the comments of other family members, that Dick really did not like his job too much. I thought this might have explained why he sometimes came home in a thunderous mood. It certainly could not have helped his demeanour at the end of a long and tiring day, in which he had to ingratiate himself to people he did not necessarily take to, as is generally the salesman's lot. I imagine he found that quite a difficult part of the job. A natural inclination not just for honesty, but for blatant, outspoken honesty, is just one of the characteristics he has passed onto his younger daughter.

When the red mist descended, School Lane was not a comfortable place to be. It was not slammed doors, I remember, so as much as a curtness of tone. Dick had a naturally loud voice. He would have made a fearsome and commanding head teacher, I thought, as I gradually drifted towards that profession myself.

On the bad days, he would not be in the house for long. He disappeared to the garage, which doubled as a workshop, where he would put to good use what appeared to my admittedly untrained eye to be very competent wood working skills. From time to time, fitments and articles of furniture would emerge that were then employed all around the house and which were to stand the test of time and the attentions of a large family.

Whether or not, on the bad days, Dick always harnessed his energies constructively remains a matter of conjecture, however. Perhaps he just beat into submission the first large block of timber that came within reach of a hand axe or a hammer until he felt better. If so, it was a singularly considerate and well judged way of restoring his equilibrium, whilst sparing the rest of the family his angst.

Joan noticed that I had been around for sufficient time to have witnessed one or two of these "moments." Instead of explaining it away with vague references to pressure at work, which was what I had expected to hear, facing me intently and speaking very deliberately, she said, "He had a difficult time in the war, Mike. He had to have shock treatment when he came out." She left it at that and returned to her kitchen tasks.

A little perplexed, I asked Chris for some more background and eventually a story was pieced together. It remained a fairly hazy affair, however. It was clear that Dick did not want to talk about what had happened to him. This was in stark contrast to my own dad's war time stories, which he was only too happy to tell to my sister and me - time after time, in fact.

Without wishing to demean or undervalue my father's efforts in any way, I don't think he would have been so forthcoming had he been witness to the full horrors of war. In fact, contracting malaria in Italy, whilst part of a radar detachment, was probably as dangerous as it got for him. He helped guide American bombers to their targets, but I think it is unlikely that he ever saw, first-hand, the resulting carnage that would have resulted from the accurate information he would have supplied, using all the latest technology. The great affection and admiration I felt for my dad were not dependent on, or in any way related to, his experiences in the RAF.

Dick Jones's war, on the other hand was a different affair altogether and his experiences would eventually be shared. He had kept pencil notes through the conflict but it was not until much later on in his life that he felt the desire, or the need, to revisit them. Was it to set the record straight, to clear his mind or to find some sort of inner peace that had hitherto been denied him? Was it a sudden urge to make them available to others whilst there was still time, or simply that he finally reached a decision that he wanted to tell his story in his own way?

I was not privy to these private thoughts and motives and I shall not try to second guess them. In the end, he recounted the events in a way that he was clearly satisfied with. Various people had a hand in producing the version that David eventually took charge of delivering, in a fashion that was readable and accessible.

So why do I feel a need to add to the original documentation at all? Firstly, I want to put his war into the context of his own full life and to place his exploits within the wider perspective of the unfolding events over which he had no control. I suppose I was intrigued by the impact such extreme experiences might have had on him and I am drawn to offer my impressions of the man I got to know and appreciate much more in his later years.

It is interesting to consider how our generation has responded to our mother's and father's experiences and to question whether we are doing enough to ensure that our own children are aware of the thread of history which connects them to the past, so that they might learn from it too.

My own generation have experienced a bit of a golden age, compared to the two that preceded us, at least. No World War Three, not even any National Service and until very recently, steadily increasing prosperity. I'm aware of the debt of gratitude we owe to our parents' efforts in the early 1940's, which have made all this possible.

As a very young man planning to take his younger daughter away from the family as soon as I could, I viewed Dick Jones as a rather intimidating figure; someone who always spoke out spontaneously and committed himself to an opinion on a range of issues at the drop of a hat. Not much taller than me, perhaps just under six feet, he was much broader backed than I was, with strong shoulders and upper arms.

He had a presence about him from the first day I met him. He moved in a stately and unhurried way. I can not imagine him running for a bus. Much more likely, he would have watched the bus pass by, strolled to the bus stop and waited patiently for the next one, without a flicker of disappointment. I never saw him rushing to do anything.

Chris says that on the day they were to go on holiday, that magical summer Saturday we all enjoyed so much each year, he would suddenly decide that there were at least half a dozen jobs that had to be attended to before he could possibly take a break - and most of them involving pieces of wood. They would then be dealt with as thoroughly as was required, before the family car, long packed up by the rest of the family, finally acquired its driver, round about tea time.

Arrival at Welsh, Cumbrian and Scottish camp sites in pitch black, either side of mid-night, was the logical consequence. Finally embedded in Broad Haven, Coniston and Wemyss Bay, his son, Malcolm, remembers that their father would entertain his children and himself, by "pulling his muscles, blowing smoke rings and flirting with waitresses in the nearby cafes!"

Family meals would have to wait until Dick was ready, too. Joan would announce that tea was served and then loudly summon those expected to attend, from distant points of the house. Everyone would be assembled – except Dad. "Dick," the cry went up. Then pause for a reply. Nothing. "Dad," then faint banging would be heard from the garage or a stooped back would suddenly be raised from the flower beds or next to the pond and into view through the hall window. He was always last to the table. Was he making an entrance? Did he do it deliberately? The master had arrived.

By comparison I was always a little shy. I found it difficult to put my personality on the line, in a "here it is, take it or leave it," sort of way. I could be disarmed by people like Dick, who apparently have no side to them, with no aspects of their personality that they were trying to hide. In his own home he was as relaxed as he was ever going to be and this is where I saw him most. Unlike me, he did not always gauge the likely reaction of a comment before he made it. He just thought out loud.

As I watched and listened to him, a little cowed at first, even over-awed on occasions, I felt for a long time that probably that is how our relationship would stay, rather remote and undeveloped. As political issues arose that we clearly had different views on, I did eventually find the courage to try him out over various issues of the day, as I gradually tried to assert myself. We eventually learnt to argue together, usually rather politely.

So who was Dick Jones and what influences had fashioned him in his early life? Why on earth did he jump at the chance of fighting for his country, whilst he was still a teenager in 1939? At the same age that I was sitting in his lounge, arranging a cushy three years as a day student at a local teacher training college, in order to tread water whilst I deliberated over what I really wanted to do next, Dick was getting into uniform and preparing for the most incredible journey, that would have marked consequences for him for the rest of his days.

2. The Early Years

Dick was born in Wallasey on June 13th 1920. He was the fourth child and only son of Captain Richard Jones and Rachel Fairburn Peattie. The Jones's were Welsh seafarers. Rachel's father came from a family of high street tailors in Edinburgh before they moved on to Glasgow. Rachel's mother was Martha Paterson and her family were Paisley coach builders. David has researched both sides of the family in some detail and his work contains fascinating stories in their own right, which fall outside the remit of this book, but which may eventually be brought to a wider audience themselves.

The Peatties lived in Elgin Drive, Wallasey, a few streets away from the Jones household. Rachel's father abandoned the home and his family was left in dire straights as a result. To make ends meet Rachel's sister took in washing for her neighbours and that is how she met Richard Jones. The Jones family were horrified, - disgusted is apparently not too strong a word for their view of the affair. He was "Going out with a washer woman!"

Relationships between the Jones and Peattie clans started off badly then fell away altogether. On such occasions as there was necessary contact between them, Rachel thought the Jones family were rude, for example by choosing to speak amongst themselves in Welsh, when in the company of their Scottish relations.

At the age of 47, Dick's father, Captain Richard Jones, died of natural causes on board his ship, the S.S. Antar and he was buried at Ross Bay Cemetery on Vancouver Island. Consequently, Dick was raised by his mother and his three older sisters, Jean, Eira and Eva. He was already effectively estranged from the Welsh antecedents who gave him his family name. Not only did he lose his dad while he was still an infant, but he lost meaningful contact with most of his Welsh relations, too.

His mother would be unable to compensate for these omissions from what might be regarded as normal family circumstances. By all accounts, Rachel herself was an austere woman, who considered, with some justification, it has to be admitted, that life had dealt her a succession of blows.

Not only had her father deserted the family. Her husband had been taken from her prematurely, leaving her seriously disadvantaged economically. She had been left to bring up four children alone in a part of the country she had not wanted to go to in the first place. Her father, also a seafarer, had originally upped sticks and left Glasgow, seduced by the promise of greater riches in the expanding port of Liverpool and taken his family with him against their wishes. Rachel never felt settled on Merseyside and the prevailing view from those who remember her was that she wore an air of bitterness and disgruntlement with her lot for the rest of her life.

The Jones family lived at 20, Monk Road in Liscard, one of the series of villages at the northern end of the Wirral, which by that time had all grown outwards and merged to form the County Borough of Wallasey. Monk Road was a typical, late Victorian, red brick, semi-detached house, built to the regular grid–iron pattern that was so common in the later years of the nineteenth century, the suburbs of their day. The Jones family home was not a particularly happy one. It was a repressed household. Rachel was a stern and firm disciplinarian. One of Dick's contemporaries remembered her as, "a perfectly genuine woman, but a bit of a dragon."

Dick's sister, Eira, remembers Dick being told off by their mother for "playing with his Meccano and making a mess and also for reading books," of all things. She apparently suggested that he might find something better to do! There is not much a child can do that is better than reading a book, surely? Rachel, described by her daughter as, "very house proud," clearly had her own agenda, which did not necessarily include improving one's literacy or the unnecessary widening of one's horizons.

From Monk Road it was a five minute walk to Manor Road School. Dick attended here until he was 9 years old, when he moved to the junior department of Wallasey Grammar School, under the direction of Miss Silvey, a renowned figure in the town at that time.

The hardship which faced the family was encapsulated in an anecdote that Dick shared with his son, David. His mother could not afford trousers for him to go to school in, so she knitted some for him. He said, not surprisingly perhaps, that he had found the experience totally humiliating.

As Dick failed to win a scholarship, his mother, eager that he should benefit from a grammar school education, tried initially to get his fees paid through Masonic lodges, firstly in Liverpool and when that was not forthcoming, the Isle of Man, to take advantage of earlier family connections with that organisation. When this ploy failed, she turned to the Mercantile Marine to secure his attendance. Dick stayed at Wallasey Grammar School courtesy of the merchant navy charities until the summer of 1936. Rachel also drew a pension from the Mercantile Marine War Widows Compensation Scheme, until her children were 16 years old.

In the same year that he started at the grammar school, Dick visited the Scout Jamboree in Arrowe Park, Birkenhead. Wallasey Grammar School had its own pack, the Second Wallasey Sea Scouts. Dick joined up at the age of eleven and the scouts became a significant influence throughout his teenage years and beyond.

Actually, it is difficult to under-estimate the importance of the sea scouts to Dick's development and up-bringing. He found in Bill Croxton the father figure he lacked at home. Skipper Croxton lived in Ormond Street, off Seaview Road and was also therefore a neighbour of the Jones family.

Not only had Dick lost his dad whilst he was still a small child, but he had never known either of his grandfathers. Having initially been surrounded by females when not at school, he became very attached to the scout master. The scouts met in the basement of the Liscard Concert Hall in Grosvenor Road, later to become the Grosvenor Ballroom. The Beatles apparently played the Grosvenor fourteen times, but they were there too late for Dick and just too early for me.

At scouts, Dick was put in Eric Harvey's crew. Eric was two years older than Dick and had already been made a coxswain. It was the start of a life long friendship. The highlights of the scouting year were the bi-annual scout camps, taken at Whitsuntide and during the summer holidays. They offered the youngsters opportunities to widen their experiences by seeing various parts of the country, often travelling from Birkenhead or Liverpool by over-night train.

Dick, pictured in the centre of this shot and by then promoted to a leadership role as coxswain, would help to organise the younger scouts at camp.

Such forays would inevitably encourage the development of a range of practical skills, plus, being able to accept responsibility, contributing to decision making as part of a group and taking the initiative when required. Amongst other trips, the scouts went to the Trossachs in 1931 and 1932, to Wensleydale in 1932, to Bath in 1933, Somerset again in 1938 and finally, as it turned out, to the Isle of Man in 1939. For families of limited means like Dick's, adventures with the scouts provided a wealth of experience as cheaply as they could do it, which in his case was probably just as well.

After he had gained the School Certificate but not matriculation, Dick left the upper fifth form in July 1936 and started to look for a job. He took with him an encouraging endorsement from the Headmaster, F.L. Allan, which made mention of his leadership qualities, as well as his good manners, efficiency and sense of responsibility.

TELEPHONE 141 WALLASEY.

**WALLASEY GRAMMAR SCHOOL,
CHESHIRE.**

23rd July, 1936.

R.H.Jones has attended this school since September 1929 and is now in an Upper Fifth Form and a candidate for the School Certificate at the examination now in progress. He has made reasonable advancement on the academic side of school life and recent Reports show that he has been working for the examination with proper industry.

He has taken a normal part in the general activities of school life playing all the school games and showing some excellence at swimming for which sport he holds his Senior House Colours. He is also a member of the school company of Sea Scouts and holds coxwain's rank which indicates some capacity for leadership. He is a well mannered boy and is likely to understand responsibility and efficiently perform the duties of the career which he takes up. I have, therefore, pleasure in recommending him.

M.A.Cantab.

F. L. Allan.

Headmaster.

Dick's reference from the headmaster at Wallasey Grammar School.

In November of the same year, Grace Brothers and Company Limited [Grace Cotton Company Limited], Old Hall Street, Liverpool, were sufficiently impressed by this reference that they appointed him as a junior clerk.

His first employment was short lived, however. By March 1937, Dick was looking for work again, armed with a written recommendation from his now former employers, who had terminated his employment when they had to close down the department in which he was operating.

By the next June Dick had found another job, this time with R.O. Edwards, a timber merchants based in Liverpool. Edwards imported hardwood timber from tropical countries through St Catherine's dock. They had a yard and offices nearby. Their products were sold as widely as possible in the port's hinterland, but largely in Lancashire itself.

Here, Dick served an apprenticeship, having been given "a hand in," as his friend, Eric Harvey, put it. One of the Jones connections, who had not lost all contact with Rachel and in spite of the frostiness in relations, was prepared to do her and her son a favour. David thinks it was likely to have been Welsh Uncle Griff John Jones, who Dick had to thank for this intervention.

With work in place, promotion at scouts and now with trips to the pub thrown in, namely the Queen's Arms, on the corner of Queen Street and Rake Lane and a mere stone's throw from scout HQ, Dick's social life was clearly on the up. Eric, Gerry Roughsedge, Bob Fish, [not a scout but a particularly close friend who lived in Harvey Road] and Mick Harris, who attended the Central School, would remain part of a close knit group for the rest of their days.

Coxswain Dick Jones on a pre-war scout camp.

Girls had also become an important part of the mix. "At this time our social life was at its best," recalled Eric. He introduced Dick to a distant cousin of his, Joan Chaddock, who lived with her younger sister, Marguerite, at 15b, Belvidere Road and after 1938, at 4, Wharfedale Road, near the Oval. "Dick was a bit of a lad for the girls," he continued. "We were having parties every day! Cousin Maisie shut the gate on him, literally, to keep her distance, after she had been out with Dick." Maisie had been staying on holiday with Eric's family, from her home in Devon.

After a bit of a sticky start in life, things were falling into place for Dick Jones. Having three older sisters doting on him as a child, must have meant he learnt early on how to communicate with women and perhaps how to get his own way, more often than not. He gained self confidence as a lively member of a mutually supportive and close gang of mates. He had a natural demeanour that was both positive and friendly. He discovered that he had a talent for getting on with members of the opposite sex, when it started to matter. He had a ready smile and he had grown to become a bit of a charmer. What could possibly go wrong? The answer, of course, was World War Two.

3. The Combatant.

One imagines that those around at the time and certainly those, "in the know," could see World War Two coming well before it actually arrived. Whether you go back as far as Germany's defeat in 1918 and the resentment caused by reparation arrangements, continued economic distress, the growth of the National Socialist Party or Hitler's coming to power, towards the end of the 1930's it was pretty obvious that a serious situation was developing.

In a remarkably candid self-assessment, the astonishingly moving museum in Berlin, Topographie de Terroir, erected inside the crumbling gates, still in situ though partly fallen, that formed the entrance to the former Gestapo headquarters, modern Germany plumps for 1933 as the key moment.

Hitler became Chancellor in January that year and set about his radical plans immediately. By July, Germany was a one party state and it was all down hill from then on. By 1938 Chamberlain was waving his piece of paper around rather forlornly, while Hitler took over in Austria and the Sudetenland in Czechoslovakia. By August 1939, Germany had already signed pacts with Italy and Russia.

Britain signed a mutual assistance pact with Poland on August 25th and a week later, on 1st September, Hitler invaded Poland. The rest, as they say, is history. Two days later, at 11.00 a.m., Britain and others declared war on Germany.

In Wallasey, even the party-goers would have noticed the descending mood as the year progressed. The Air Raid Precautions organisation [ARP] took over the ground floor of the Liscard Concert Hall, where the scouts met. Here they amassed gas masks, to protect citizens from the poison gas that they feared could be dropped from enemy planes.

This is the point at which Dick takes up his own story. The pencil notes in a reporter's notebook, start to record his view of events and for the first time we have first hand information to go on. Commuting to work on the ferry boat from Seacombe to Liverpool in 1939, he discussed with his friend, Mick Harris, the pros and cons of joining up then with the Territorial Army as opposed to waiting for the eventual inevitability of conscription.

In the spring of 1939 the 149th Royal Horse Artillery [Territorial Army] was founded in Hoylake in West Wirral. The scout rover crew, Mick Harris, Gerry Roughsedge, Eric Harvey and Dick Jones all signed up together. Dick was still an eighteen year old.

> *"We did not join because of an over-whelming patriotic urge.*
> *Our reasons were roughly as follows:-*
> *1. There seemed to be more chance of survival in a 25 pounder*
> *   artillery regiment than in an infantry regiment.*
> *2. As it was local we would know many friends.*
> *3. We might learn to ride.*

> *4. We were told that our employer would have to release us for the annual summer camp, as well as any holidays we would normally get. As most of us only had a week's holiday a year, this was attractive."*

Learning to ride would have been a bit of a long shot. The Royal Artillery no longer used horses to pull guns around, keeping them only for ceremonial purposes. The "holiday" idea was shortly to go out of the window for obvious reasons and for all the training that followed on 25 pounder guns, there was a nasty shock waiting in that direction, too. At least, for the time being, they were all friends together.

Eric Harvey added, "We all kept up our connections with the scouts right up to the time we set off for Egypt. Conscription was for those reaching the age of 21 and lasted for six months so that was to be a very large break in our career prospects or so we feared. As Mick and I had our 21st birthdays in that August it was important that we joined the Territorial Army, or similar, to be exempt from conscription and Dick joined up in sympathy. Once committed it became a bit obscure as to the benefit of our actions with the war starting so soon. Let it be said that I never regretted our choice – we started off with all our old friends and by the time people got posted to other units we had had at least learned the ropes in a brotherly atmosphere."

He continued, "The Hoylake HQ for the regiment was in a set of hutments built in a field off a lane to the rear of the railway station, which led nowhere except to the new golf club house [which became the officers' mess] whilst the old club house became the base for the gas sentries – in which all three of us started our military careers."

New recruits were billeted in many of the large Victorian houses in Hoylake and West Kirby, though some were allowed to stay at home if they were local enough. Training took place in the evenings until they were "embodied" - apparently a TA term for being mobilised – and this took place just before the outbreak of hostilities.

The day before war was declared, the regiment was mustered at 9.00 a.m. on Saturday 2nd September. The rover crew's lives would never be the same again. Barrack life began and full time training commenced. Mick, Gerry and Dick all became signallers.

It must have seemed like the training went on for ever. As well as Hoylake itself, they attended training camps in Rugeley, Stafford, Great Malvern and Stourbridge between September 1939 and October 1940. That's fourteen months learning about big guns. They must have known them inside out.

In March 1941 they embarked at Avonmouth onto the Reino del Pacifico, bound for Egypt, the very long way round. Built in 1931 for the Pacific Steam Navigation Company, she was employed as a troop ship between 1939 and 1946. The plan was to join an Atlantic convoy in Clydemouth, but she hit a wreck in the Severn Estuary almost immediately and was diverted to the Mersey for repairs to her propeller. This gave the rover crew an unexpected three weeks fire watching duties on Liverpool warehouses.

Having benefited from the relative protection afforded to a trans-Atlantic convoy, she almost made it to the American coast before turning back and heading eastwards towards Freetown, in Sierra Leone, a British colony on the west coast of Africa. Completing this great arc through the ocean was the safest way to avoid attack from German U-boats and warships.

Continuing around the western periphery of the continent, she passed the Cape of Good Hope just in time to meet the worst storm seen there in seventy years. That was quite something. Eric almost visibly shuddered as he sat and thought about it from the comfort of his armchair. It was over seventy years ago and no doubt as clear as day. "The waves were enormous. It was difficult to see how we were going to get through it."

This is how it was described by another commentator, E.W. Capleton, "The scene was one of great moving mountains of water….at the last minute the leading edge of the wave would lift the stern and bury the bows in a mass of white foam; as the crest reached amidships it so lifted the stern that the propellers raced in mid-air."[p.53]

After eight weeks on board [presumably including the Liverpool diversion] they must have been so pleased to reach Durban. Dick and Eric were really impressed with what they saw of South Africa, during their fortnight's stay, "A beautiful country and masses of fresh fruit." It must have provided such welcome relief after the traumas of the voyage.

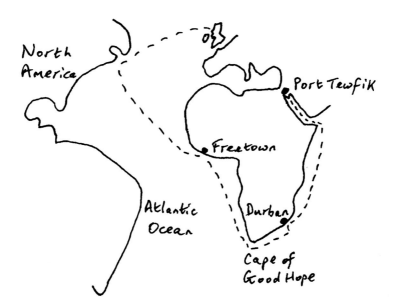

Only too soon they were back at sea, on the Nieuw Amsterdam this time. Constructed in 1937 as the most recent flag ship of the Holland America Line, she too had become a troop ship for the war effort. Their course took them up the east coast of Africa and eventually via the Red Sea to Port Tewfik. By train, they were taken to Cairo and then onwards to Mena Camp. Twelve miles out from the centre by tram, on the outskirts of the city and within view of the pyramids, Mena Camp had been used for training by the Allies during World War One as well.

The protection the friends thought might have been afforded to them by their proximity to 25 pounder guns soon evaporated at Mena. They were diverted to train on 2 pounder anti-tank guns in their place and they were now to be part of the 149th Anti-Tank Regiment, Royal Artillery, potentially in an altogether more exposed situation on the battlefield.

Disappointment in this area might have been partly assuaged by life at the camp, as Eric remembered. "Mena Camp was well established with units with loos, playing fields, and water laid on. Dick played hockey. We visited Cairo once a month, where we saw "Gone with the Wind." We bought macaroni cheese there. It was a chaotic place, though. We were warned about thieves who would cut through our watch straps, for example."

Dick, while he was at the Mena training camp near Cairo.

The fleshpots of Cairo, macaroni and weepy films would not distract them for long. By rail they moved on to Alexandria at the mouth of the Suez Canal and from there by destroyers HMS Jarvis and HMS Harty to Tobruk in Libya. Eric was surprised that on arrival, "We were asked to put on our gym shoes. It was to make us a little more sure-footed for the cat walk across the sunken ships that formed a barrier at the harbour."

Mediterranean Sea

Tobruk Alexandria Mena Port Tewfiq

Cairo

Libya Egypt

"We arrived in the desert. The Aussies made us tea. Rations were limited, two pints of water a day, bread, bully beef and no vegetables. Our defences were not very coherent and we had to set up our own."

Dick became separated from his friends as their deployment in the desert took shape. On the 21st of September, Dick became part of the force that would take up front line positions relieving batteries of Australian anti tank regiments, amongst others. They had become the 70th Division of the Eighth Army, the famous Desert Rats and more particularly, the Rats of Tobruk, initially named as such by the traitor and propagandist, Lord Haw-Haw. The name stuck, to be adopted by the Allies themselves.

The conflict in North Africa had gone the same way as the other major theatres up to this time, that is to say, badly. In mainland Western Europe, on the Russian front and in the desert, German forces had generally prevailed. Britain was extremely keen to keep control of the Suez Canal and the North African campaign that Dick was becoming part of was largely about thwarting Hitler's intention to wrestle control of the strategic waterway from the Allies. Australian, New Zealander, Indian, Czechoslovakian and Polish troops were also deployed to stop this happening.

Tobruk itself was captured from the Italians in January 1941. It became a beleaguered garrison but it was also an enclave that tied up German resources, which might otherwise have been concentrated further east. Also, it remained open as an access point for reinforcements and supplies and as a possible springboard site for future attacks. Rommel, commander of the Afrika Corps and nicknamed the Desert Fox, was determined that it would be overcome.

General Auchinleck, the British commander, decided on a three pronged attack on German forces, involving movement west from Egypt to coincide with a break out from Tobruk. The operation was code-named Crusader and planned for the 18th of November, but delayed in part for two days by poor weather.

> *"Our job was to break out of Tobruk and capture El Duda on the main road between Benghazi and El Alamein……In the end we*

*had to take the position ourselves, due to the delay of the main
forces. This culminated in an exhilarating five mile dash to
capture our objective on the 25th November."*

El Duda was just 15 miles south east of Tobruk. An observation post on a ridge and on
the road that by-passed Tobruk, it was fought over time after time, as the Allies tried to
break Rommel's line of communications. Although Crusader was eventually a success,
when the victorious Eighth Army entered Tobruk to break the siege on the 8th of
December, Rommel would finally gain control of the garrison in June 1942, though even
that, of course, would not be the end of the story.

The internet is just bursting with accounts of battles from the Second World War. It is a
massive area of interest, with many contributions by historians, still arguing over
minutiae and motives. Researchers extract the last drop of detail out of events and chat
rooms abound in which modern theorists exchange observations. Most poignantly, the
memories of old soldiers have been added, often with the help of the next generation. It is
all there for further investigation, if required. My inclination here is towards
simplification. I want to understand what happened, but not to get too bogged down in
the detail. To this end, I am lucky to have Dick's original version to draw on.

> *"Our gun position was a very open one and we moved back to a better
> position on the 26th November 1941. We remained in this position
> during the 27th November, spending a gruelling and nerve shattering
> day due to the enemy's concentrated machine gun, mortar and
> artillery fire.*
>
> *About 5 o'clock our Sergeant, Sergeant Faulkner, was blown in half
> by a mortar which landed not ten yards from my trench.*
>
> *Strangely enough he and I had an argument as to which of us should occupy
> the trench he lost his life in. Our trenches were barely a foot deep
> surrounded by sandbags. We buried Sergeant Faulkner that night. We had*

no crosses so we placed his hat on his rude grave."

Concerned about the exposed location they had found themselves in, they moved again, digging deeper trenches this time and taking advantage of a dried up river bed [known in the desert as a wadi]. Reinforcements were expected in the form of recently disembarked New Zealanders and the morning of the 29th November remained very quiet.

> *"I remember washing and shaving that morning and cooking a large breakfast. It was comforting to feel that we were no longer isolated and that our forces were near at hand. Yes, and I was clean again. My face and hands were no longer covered with sand and dirt. I was sure that for a time slit trench grovelling was over. There was even talk of relief very shortly but I did not bank too strongly on this."*

A captain and a lieutenant from the Essex Regiment had joined them in the wadi and they had noticed German tents being erected on a distant ridge. Around lunch time they were suddenly under attack.

> *"Speedily we mounted the gun and prepared to meet the danger that faced and threatened us. There were forty German tanks in all and our small guns could hardly cope with such a number. As quickly as we fired and disabled tanks more came on with panther-like dashes, slowly advancing. We knew that unless we could obtain tank support, it was just a matter of time. Machine gunners put up a wonderful display, but had the disheartening experience of seeing our bullets ricocheting from the armour plating of the enemy's tanks. It was a horror-striking sight watching our shields being ripped to pieces by machine gun bullets. First the shield was riddled with bullets, and then the traversing mechanism was out of action. Finally the gun commenced slipping back in the pit. A sharp cry from our layer, Tom Forshaw, "My God, I'm hit!" and his slumping out of the seat distracted us. How we dragged him out of that pit without being hit I do not know. We lifted him as gently as possible into a slit trench, puzzled that there was no sign of blood anywhere. On examination, we discovered that some bullets had torn his clothing and even lodged in his coat but apart from that, there was nothing really wrong. He seemed to be suffering from shock.*
>
> *A loud explosion behind us told us our gun had fired its last shot. We found the two infantry officers I mentioned firmly planted in our trench with a lieutenant, who, besides taking up half the room infuriated me with his lazy affected drawl. We asked for orders and were informed that everything was under control. I doubted this but could not act on my own without the permission of my superiors. The afternoon drew on. We huddled there waiting and hoping for tank support. It never came and gradually the noise and opposition ceased, as each point was put out of commission. Near us strange tanks were rumbling. My every bone was*

cramped and numb. I was dying for a smoke and was out of cigarettes. At last the sound of German voices told us it was the end. It was no use doing anything now. A tank on the ridge kept pumping bullets just over our heads and trying to get out was certain death.

He was a puny little German who ordered us out of the trench. His automatic looked absurdly heavy in his small hand. Thus it was that I became a prisoner of war. I was to enter a strange new life, which can break you if you let it. I have seen many die of a broken heart, hunger and illness. I have seen and felt such misery, that suffering and sordidness no longer impress me. Like a frog living in a stagnant pool, I cannot feel the slime or smell the stink.

Crawling, running, we made our way through the German lines. All the way, we were shelled by our own 25 pounders. My last glimpse was a German staff car, which we had shot up a few a days before. Finally we reached the German lines and I was amazed at the number of British lorries they were using."

I make it that from the day that the regiment was mustered on the 2nd September 1939, Dick spent 2 years and 19 days training for and travelling to his initial position to defend that first front line. He was then an active combatant for just 2 months and 8 days, although as the break out from Tobruk did not actually happen until the 20th November, Dick might have been considered himself to be in more direct mortal danger for the nine day period thereafter, before becoming a prisoner of war for the next 3 years and 9 months.

Being moved off the 25 pounder guns whilst still at Mena, which would provide the aerial bombardment from a slightly safer distance and then being transferred to the smaller, more manoeuvrable 2 pounders, which were going to be deployed decidedly closer to the enemy, must have been a jaw dropping moment, as the reality of the adjustment and its implications had sunk in.

To then be part of a push towards enemy territory as part of a wider offensive, which never materialised in the way that was planned, not to receive the back up troops they had been told were on the way and being forced to claim and make as secure as possible a decidedly exposed entrenchment, one can only imagine what was going through their minds.

If they could have seen the overall picture of repeated advances and retreats, the skirmishes and the briefly successful "hit and run" night time assaults that characterised the fluid and ever changing pattern of the tank battles that typified desert warfare, they would no doubt have been even less confident of getting out of there alive.

They ended up as an exposed and under strength prong of an advance that was unlikely to succeed. They were outnumbered, outgunned and outmanoeuvred. Dick's time in combat was cut short, but he survived it. The carnage that was taking place all around him, so carefully documented since, reminds us what a lottery survival had become.

It depended, in his particular case, on the outcome of a brief argument with a comrade over trench occupancy, someone who presumably pulled rank on him when it came to the crunch and unknowingly condemned himself to death. Life hung by such threads as these. It is so difficult to imagine what it must have been like to be there to experience it all first-hand.

In his own account, Dick says that the details of the battle he was involved in are spelt out in E.W. Capleton's book, "Shabash – 149, The war story of the 149th Regiment R.A." Matching up the two, it is clear that Dick has chosen to spare his readers some of the grim details that made up his experiences on that last day of "freedom." My reading of it is that Dick must have been part of "A" Troop, as they dug in at El Duda. At that moment, Rommel, himself, was only a few miles away at El Adem, plotting Dick's and his colleagues' demise.

"A" Troop had four two-pounder gun emplacements dug in behind two companies of the Essex Regiment and in front of the British tanks and of the big guns. German tanks attacked at 13.50 that afternoon. The Allied tanks fired over the heads of the gunners, but they had little effect on the oncoming Panzers. As Brigadier Williton put it, quoted in Capleton's account, "It was pitiful to see our 2 pounder shells bouncing off the enemy tanks." [p.115]

Capleton himself describes what happened next. ""A" Troop's battle was of doomed men. Sergeant Cheshire's gun was enveloped in the smoke of two direct hits, before bursting into flames. A little further away, on another gun, Sergeant Joe Young and Bim Harrison died at their posts….whilst Tom Sowerby lay across the trail of the gun mortally wounded. Soon… the guns fell silent. When the smoke lifted a great semi-circle of Panzers sat on the position."[p.115] All four emplacements had been disabled by enemy fire and most of the soldiers manning the other three guns were presumably dead.

It would be at this point that Dick was taken prisoner, as the Germans cleared the trenches and dug in themselves. The urgently requested reinforcements did not arrive until the next day, too late for Dick, in one respect, though who knows what could have happened, had he made it back to his own lines, as some behind him were to do that night.

There must come a time, surely, in the face of such adversity, when being taken prisoner suddenly looks like a comparatively favourable option. How sickening though, to lay down your arms and allow those that you have just been firing at to humble you, knowing too, that they have only recently killed and wounded your friends and comrades. Dick was 21 years old. His adult life had barely begun, but he was already witness to sights that would be enough to haunt you for the rest of your days.

In the year of my own 21st birthday, I toured Cornwall and Devon in my friend's dad's car, went abroad by train with Chris for the first time in August and spent the autumn half term youth hostelling in the Lake District as part of a group of eleven, swanning around in four different vehicles. The contrasting situations would not have crossed my consciousness at all at the time. I was having far too much fun.

Back home in Wallasey in 1941, Dick's twenty first birthday presents remained unclaimed. His mother eventually disposed of them. Neither did she retain any letters home that she received from him. In fact, it seems that she did not expect him to return at all.

<u>4. Prisoner of War.</u>

"Gerry, taken all round, showed consideration and put the coatless in tents. It was very cold. We were searched, and I lost most of my possessions, including my wallet and photographs. In the early hours of the morning we were turned over to the Italians, who marched us all night, sometimes this way and sometimes that. Eventually, exhausted, we arrived at El-Adem Aerodrome, which looked the worse for wear due to commando raids."

Changing hands more than once during the North Africa campaigns, El-Adem was an Italian air force base before the war. Captured again by the British, it was largely reconstructed in 1942 and used by the United States Nine Air Force. Operated by the British after the war up until 1970, it became a less than popular venue during post-war National Service. More than one web site contributor, remembering those days, insisted that El-Adem means "the end," in Arabic. You can guess what they thought of it as a posting.

Rather bizarrely, El Adem made the news in Britain on one other notable occasion. When King George VI died in 1952, his daughter, Princess Elizabeth, was in Uganda. Her BOAC flight back from Entebbe stopped at El Adem Airport for 58 minutes, so that it could be refuelled before progressing to London, to allow the new queen to begin her reign.

"Lorries arrived into which we were packed. The rush of the cool morning air freshened me considerably after the night's long march.

Our first prison camp was the remains of an old farmhouse and consisted of a cobbled courtyard surrounded by four walls. Opposite the entrance some rickety sheds stood and on the right were some buildings used as offices. Again we were searched and nearby allowed to quench our thirst. My hunger wore off by then and a few hitches at my belt kept it at bay for another hour or two. I was divested of a few remaining treasures, a fountain pen, and a pair of scissors, leaving me with shirt, tin hat and a handkerchief as my possessions.

It was hard to realise what had happened during the past few days, but I had all day to think. Sleep came very easily and I dozed and dreamed for many hours.

I realised that my future life would not be my own. I would grow accustomed to sentries guarding me, barbed wire surrounding me, a prey to the whims of the enemy who could please themselves whether I lived or died.

They were surprised at our leather jackets and tried to glean information from us by means of cigarettes and sympathy. The long day passed tempers grew strained and hunger gnawed at our stomachs, which had been peckish but never hungry. At long last a biscuit and a tin of bully [Italian] between two were issued. Italian sentries opened our tins and we made the best of our sparse repast, washed down with water. I looked about for sleeping quarters but the rumble of lorries told me my travels would begin again.

Our next camp was a field, where many prisoners of war were marshalled, some having been there all day. Here I met with many friends and spent half the night talking to George Cheshire. He had been digging graves at a German hospital and according to his reports he had been treated very well. Our plan was to go out there next day, if only to fill our stomachs.

After a cold damp night huddled beneath wet ground sheets, lorries drew up outside the wire. Thinking it was the working party I have mentioned, we immediately got in them. My thoughts were filled with the possibility of a little extra food. Hell, I was hungry! But we were wrong. Bully beef and biscuits were issued to us in the trucks. We made ourselves as comfortable as possible under the circumstances. After a fast trip, we found ourselves wending our way down the escarpment at Derna – a wonderful road and a credit to engineering skill."

There is something beguiling about some of Dick's observations, commenting as he does on the nature of the landscape he is passing through and making appreciative observations on the quality of road construction. You might have expected that he would be totally self obsessed by this point and oblivious to where he was or what it looked like. Perhaps it served simply to temporarily take his mind off his predicament.

Trying to put myself in his position, I think it's likely that I would already have been ill. An all night march, a day time sleep in an old farmyard, a trip in the back of a lorry, a cold, damp night in a field, another lorry journey and all on a diet restricted in every way. I would probably have been developing pneumonia by then.

As a child, I was put on a lengthy low fat diet for acute stomach pains and I received heat ray treatment - for general weediness, I think - and I was a bit undernourished and susceptible to respiratory infections. Even by twenty one, I know I would not have faced up well to any prolonged hardship of this kind. You had to be tough to take this from the outset.

The penny must have dropped very early on as these men adjusted to this new life. They were not just going to have to be physically equipped but mentally resolute to survive and that was in addition to whatever extra dangers circumstance might throw at them.

Mediterranean Sea

Barce
Benghazi
Derna
El Adem
Libya

They were still only about a hundred miles or so from Tobruk and less than half the way towards their destination, the port of Benghazi. Now known as the Libyan Coastal Highway, the main road to Benghazi and beyond was built by the Italian colonists and opened by Mussolini in 1937. Derna is a sizable coastal town between the Mediterranean Sea and this green and well forested upland part of Eastern Libya. As in the Second World War, its situation on this major strategic line of communication was important during the more recent conflict to oust Colonel Gaddafi.

> *"Derna is a rather pretty town: its white buildings bathed in sunshine. We drew into some sort of camp and there waited for something to happen. Civilians fetched water and were only too anxious to strip us of anything we happened to possess. Egyptian pounds, gold watches, and every precious jewel, are of little value when you are hungry, not knowing when the next bite is coming from. And a loaf of bread, pot of jam and a few cigarettes were eagerly taken for an Egyptian pound. Rolex jewelled watches were exchanged for mere trifles, considering their value. It seems impossible that men should be driven to these ends but hunger and thirst do queer things to you. The animal instinct prevails and the luxuries of civilisation are of little importance, as long as you can sink your teeth into solid food.*
>
> *Once again and feeling tired out, we humped along in a stupor, not caring what happened. No glimmer of hope could I see. Every minute despair seemed to get deeper and deeper. Memories came crowding back, haunting and tantalising me. It seemed I had only to stretch out my hand, to grasp and enjoy them again. It rained hard that night and this did not help matters. At long last the rain ceased and the moon, as if to cheer our bedraggled misery, peeped through the cloud, throwing a pale light on the hard wet road. The spinning wheels tore through the night. Scenery here was magnificent, and I took notice once again. The road wound in and out of the hills through forests, looking black as black in the moonlight. It was pleasant to watch a bit of scenery again. It helped to take things off my mind; racing through the night, chugging up*

mountainsides, pelting helter-skelter downhill, with the dark firs rising loftily on each side. But short-lived, was our view of scenery and soon we were on the road again and heading for Bachi, near Benghazi."

Mention of Bachi had me stumped for a time, but it appears that the town formerly known as Barce [and Barca] has become better known as Al Marj, during the time that has elapsed since. That settlement is firmly on the road from Derna to Benghazi, so I think that is probably problem solved. In 1963, an earthquake here killed 300 people.

"The night was spent at Bachi Barracks, arriving there cold and hungry. The commandant issued us with a tin of bully between two, and a biscuit per man, a generous gesture at such a late hour. Eating, so seldom now, was a pleasure and each dry morsel, each tough string of horseflesh tasted so delicious, so succulent.

Feeling a little cheerier, I bedded down. 4 a.m. I woke up, with shoulders aching, legs stiff and almost numb with cold. A torrent of rain beat down on the roof and the moon shining through the windows glinted on deep puddles on the wooden floor. Sleep being out of the question, I huddled in a dry spot waiting for the dawn, itching to be on the move again, eager and hopeful that somewhere, someday, I should be able to rest my weary body.

Morning saw us bumping and jostling towards Benghazi, finally stopping at an Italian barracks. From the outside it appeared a home from home. The walls were white and of mosque-like construction. The sheds were airy and meant shelter from the rain. Outside the rather flat town of Benghazi stretched inwards from the sea.

Altogether a week was spent in this clearing depot, the memory of which I shall not forget. The days were warm and we spent them sleeping. The nights were a sharp contrast and were so cold that sleeping was impossible. We huddled together, taking nightly shifts from sleeping in outside position. South Africans, apparently captured with full kit, slept well and never offered us a blanket to keep the draught out. The cold hard ground struck right through our bodies. Occasionally we found wood and while it lasted huddled round its warm glow.

But our next stop was Italy. There were permanent camps, veritable Butlins holiday resorts, where prisoners lived in comfort and ease; food was plentiful and you even received a Red Cross parcel every week. With this happy life ahead we stood the appalling stench of latrines – great holes in the ground, where one perched on poles to complete one's ablutions. Cigarettes were scarce and rations were bare. I was always hungry and not very clean. With no soap, washing was a miserable business."

The main Italian holding depot for prisoners of war waiting for crossings to Italy was located a few miles outside Benghazi near Bernina Airport. It was an infamous location. Overcrowded and lacking resources, rations were considerably less than adequate. Men lay flat out to conserve energy and blackouts, through lack of nutrition, were common. Dysentery was a frequent affliction in the camp. Increasing numbers of skeletal POWs were eventually noted arriving at Italian camps, through this main Libyan transit camp and exit port.

As preparations were being made to ship Dick and his comrades to Italy, the war they were being extricated from in North Africa carried on behind them, of course. Auchinleck's insistence that the garrison at Tobruk made every effort to take the El Duda ridge, which had cost Dick his liberty [but which could also inadvertently have saved his life], was actually realised just a day or two later. The whole area would fall again to the Germans in 1942, before eventual allied triumph, following Montgomery's successes at El Alamein later on in the same year and again in 1943.

> "*8th December 1941. At last the long awaited day arrived and we were transported to Benghazi docks. I sighed with relief: conditions could not be much worse than at this place. How I was mistaken and how insignificant the hardship of the past compared with the difficulties to come. The Padre's last words to us were, "Your only chance left is to be intercepted by a British destroyer and liberated."*
>
> *Our ship was a cargo boat and we were the cargo. Packed tight in the holds of the ship, sealed and battened down with no facilities or conveniences, we said goodbye to Libya, Egypt and all that we remembered during our short stay.*
>
> *Our journey was to be of two days' duration and we made ourselves as comfortable as possible. Many men had contracted dysentery. How those lads suffered, standing for hours in queues as one by one they were allowed to use the latrines. Night-time: even this convenience ceased and our only air supply came from the cracks in the hatch covers. Soon air became scarce and the atmosphere foul. Perspiration ran down my back. My whole body was clammy. As the long night drew on men became desperate. The fog of stale air and the stench of unwashed bodies was almost unbearable. My head began to throb and as each hour dragged along, the throbbing pain driving sledgehammer blows grew worse. To add to our discomfort, oil-drums were lowered to use as latrines and the stink of them was nauseating.*
>
> *Did I sleep that night or was I drugged? My sense of time and place had left me. I lay dead and lifeless, sweat running off me and between nightmare dreams I was able to sympathise with the suffering of those around me. Smoking was impossible and nobody dared light up, as there*

would have been severe trouble. This was a different type of war. No drums, no pageantry, no colour, just silent suffering, helpless, and yet hope glimmered even now. Shortly we would wake up and it would only have been a bad dream.

Day broke at last. Some hatches were opened and air came in at last. Slowly my head cleared. I tried to stand and for the first time in my life my legs failed to support me. But I did not want to sleep. My body was too weary for sleep. I lay dreaming, thinking of home. The 9th December. Everybody is looking forward to Christmas. Last year I was so happy. Christmas leave, if we managed to get through our firing camp. A growing friendship for Teddy, long teas at the Turf Café, dances at the Conservative Club, invites to tea, dates and entanglements with the fair sex and a deepening friendship with Dorothy. And yet last year with all it's rounds of activity, I was dissatisfied and had a feeling I was not doing my best for my country.

Well, I had found adventure and it did not feel so good as it reads in books. I heard that America had entered the war. At last, I thought. It cannot last much longer. Bound to be home next Christmas. So I lay there dreaming without an ounce of energy and I did not care much."

What's the time? "Two o'clock," somebody volunteered. Above I could see a little sky. Another night and not much to look forward to. A dull boom startled me. The engine stopped. Everything was suddenly blown to smithereens. Fascinated and inactive I watched the hatches blown skywards, saw them turn round slowly in the air and come down. They crashed near me. I was shivering with fear. There were men on those hatches not five feet from me, dreaming the same as I was and now their dreams were over, their lives gone. Ron Cordingly, Jackson, Tom Davies, John Grogan: they would never see home again. I hoped they never knew.

At first, after my shivering had died down, I was stupefied and then the animal instinct of self-preservation came back to me. Five minutes ago I could not stand: now fear had given me strength. There was panic in that hold. To get out, back on deck – see whether there was a chance – that was the main thing. Ladders – yes there were ladders – but how to get on them? The water was rising quickly down there; the lower hold was half full already. I looked around me. There were several men pinioned under girders. Not much chance of helping them. Arms, legs and torsos floated around and around. But there were men alive down there. I slung a couple of ropes down and made them fast. I managed to help a couple of chaps up and immediately lost them. The water was barely six feet from our own hold. I must get out. I fought my way to a ladder. The person before me kept treading on my hands. I was probably treading on the chap below me.

At last on deck, the sky above me. Land was but three miles off and the sea was calm.

Three miles, I said to myself. Could I swim it? I was quite a strong swimmer but after the energy sapping days lately, I had my doubts. It would take at least three hours provided there was no current. The ship might on the other hand go down under me, and it was better to have a crack. Then I saw somebody with a raft and asked if I might join the party. O.K. was the reply. The raft was slung over and my unknown friends jumped over with it. I was the last to go. I hauled myself on the gunwhale and then for some unknown reason I cast a glance at the bridge behind. There was an officer beckoning us all to come to the stern. Suddenly my mind changed and my head cooled. I realised the slight margin of success jumping over the side held, and the impossibility of my reaching the far shore. I bustled my way through panic-stricken men, some tearing off their clothes and jumping over. The sight of their panic calmed me. I decided to throw my lot in with the ship.

The day was calm and our ship did not appear to be sinking any more. All the men had been ordered to the stern. Several Italians were shot by a German officer who had taken charge of the ship. Our "brave" Italian captain was the first to leave the ship, accompanied by many "brave" officers, soldiers and sailors! Another lifeboat had been lowered but in the confusion and over anxiety to board it had capsized with the loss of all lives.

Our only course was to wait and see. In the meantime I looked around me for any friends but only succeeded in finding George Cheshire. Tom Summerfield was nowhere to be found. But I was not worried for they could be anywhere. The panic had in some way subsided though the sights that met my eyes turned me sick.

Our engines were still working and the German officer was endeavouring to pilot the ship towards the shore and possibly beach her. An Italian plane soared overhead and a destroyer fussed about laying depth charges.

With engines operating and propellers thrashing, disaster after disaster occurred in the water. Men on rafts were drawn towards the propellers and as each wicked blade came over, it crushed and maimed everything within its reach. The screams of the maimed and the dying made me wince and thank God I had not obeyed my first impulse. Some men could not stand the suspense and in a desperate bid threw themselves over the side to meet their death beneath the steel blades of the propellers.

I met a South African some months afterwards by the name of George O'Neil who was saved from this death and picked up by the captain's boat.

Then a strange thing occurred, be it fate or pure luck. The sea, a comparative calm, was whipped by a sudden wind, which blew landwards. I prefer to think it was the hand of God, which came to help us – we who were so helpless. Our ship, which was waterlogged and motionless, was slowly moving towards the land and not out to sea, as we feared.

The coast of this strange land, which we learned later was Greece, epic of many stories, grave of many men in this war, was very rugged. I shuddered at the thought of our helpless hulk being smashed to pieces on those cruel crags.

Gradually, yard by yard, our ship floundered towards the rocks. On top of a steep cliff there was a small town or village, and what seemed to be a sea wall to prevent the rolling sea from eating into the land. Under this wall was a narrow strip of beach – well not a beach – but compared with the rest of the coast to right and left was comparatively clear of rocks and crags. This one spot was the only one on the coast where we stood the best chance of survival.

Our thanks were due to a German officer said to be an engineer, who by using the engines managed to keep the ship side on and floating towards stretch of beach. At last the climax came, fifty yards from the shore; crunching and crashing over shoals of rocks, which seemed to tear the bottom out of us. We held ourselves in suspense and prayed to God to lodge us safely in that one spot where we might stand some slight chance of survival from an unwanted and watery grave.

I was prepared to spend the rest of my days cooped up in the barbed wire confines of a concentration camp if only my life would be spared.

How precious is life. How dear even this present existence. What untold sacrifices man will make when faced with death. He clutches at the remotest chance, clings to the wispiest reed of existence, if the fates will permit the blood to flow through his body, the breath to fill his lungs. I and my comrades struck a forlorn picture with eager anxious faces, watching a small stretch of beach, praying that some hidden power would settle our floating coffin in that limited space. Tension strong, our faces winced as we crashed and shuddered over every reef.

I believe it was the will of God and no one will convince me otherwise. He was with us that day and out of the valley of the shadow of death He brought us to safety. With a lurch we settled on the beach. Our vessel lifted and crashed, shattering the frayed nerves of each of us. We feared that the suffering plates would not hold out and we held our breaths as with decreasing lurches our ship settled in her grave.

The major climax passed. We turned and gave three cheers to the officer engineer and thanked God for his mercy and deliverance.

More problems presented themselves. How to get away from this luckless hulk? How to plant my feet firmly on the shores of Greece as others before had sought to leave that poor land.

Looking over the sides I saw the angry sea swirling around the dark ugly rocks, rearing their heads out of a foam-flecked kaleidoscope of blue and white: common sense told me that it was impossible to live down there. I decided to wait for something to happen and made myself comfortable.

The incoming sea crashed against our vessel, waves driving on us until we were drenched and no longer cared. As each wave lashed our carcass shook in its death agony. How the creations of man trembled before the furies of nature. Night fell at last, and with its cheerless pal misery gripped me. The hopes which were so high, gradually receded to despair. I heard the futile efforts of the brave to reach the shore by swimming. Nelson's chairs had been erected but had been found useless. Finally ropes were attached to the top deck and men were told to slide down them.

George Cheshire was violently sick but after a while recovered. About 9 o'clock we waited to go over the side. At last it was only two from my turn, my heart pounding against my ribs, tasteless saliva coming into my mouth. I tried to control myself. I often wondered who those two men were who went before me. All I heard was their screams, as losing hold of the slippery rope they were pounded to death in the merciless combination of angry sea and cruel rocks.

Hauling myself up on the gunwhale and holding on to a stanchion, for she was by no means steady, I prepared for the last bid for safety. If it failed I hoped the suffering would not be for too long.

An anxious sergeant told me to say OK when I had reached the shore and exclaimed, "For God's sake hang onto the rope." With these thoughts in my mind and prayers on my lips, I made ready for the water chute. Entwining my legs and arms round the greasy strands; down and down into the darkness I slid and then stopped. My journey was by no means over but I had reached the extremity of the rope's curve and all that remained was to crawl hand over hand. This I did and finally reached the surging water. I lowered my feet and the moment they touched the water they were swept away dragging my whole body. I hung on like grim death, knowing that to leave go meant a ghastly end. The wave subsided for a while but another came tearing at my body once more. I soon learned that in between waves I could edge my way gradually along the rope. This I did fearing that I would be caught unawares only holding on with one hand.

When the waves hit me it took all my strength to retain my hold. In the distance a swinging lantern flickered and glimmered. At last I reached the rocks, ugly crags which tore and cut my bruised knees. A last struggle, a last effort to make the few remaining yards across rock and angry sea. Yard by yard I clinged frantically to my lifeline. At last my feet struck solid ground and I hauled myself out of the sea."

In spite of the frequency with which I have read this account I still find the whole episode not just frightening, but spellbinding. After what Dick had been subjected to in the desert, the least he might have reasonably hoped for was that his captors would respect the conventions that govern responsibilities to prisoners of war and that a straightforward crossing of the Mediterranean Sea might precede internment in mainland Europe.

He was afforded no such luck. The camps prior to departure were overcrowded and under- resourced leaving the captives seriously undernourished, presumably making what followed doubly difficult to take in and respond to. By this stage I was well aware of the personal resilience you would have had to call on to get through.

The story of the attack and the shipwreck off the coast of Greece is well documented, although not every detail is consistent. This interpretation represents what I hope is a consensus from the range of available contributions to the ongoing discussion.

The Italian 6,310 ton ship was built in 1939 in Amsterdam and named the Jason. She is also referred to as the Jantzen in some reports. Newman Robinson, in his account entitled, "In The Bag," calls her the San Sebastian. Requisitioned by the Italian Navy, she was actually re-named the Sebastiano Venier. Leaving Benghazi on the 8th December 1941 with 2,000 allied prisoners and with one escort vessel, she was bound for Bari in Italy. She was not flying a POW flag when she was torpedoed the next day by the British submarine, HMS Porpoise, off the Greek coast and five miles south of Navarino in the Peloponnese.

The log of the Porpoise shows that she was in a position 36 degrees 43 minutes north and 21 degrees and 34 minutes east when she sighted the ship at 14.25 and she fired 4 torpedoes at her at 14.35. Reports indicate that both the freighter and the Italian torpedo boat escort had seen the periscope of the Porpoise, but to no avail.

Hit between holds one and two on the starboard side, the hold covers on the Sebastiano Venier reached mast height before falling on to men trying to escape from the holds themselves. Only five men came out of the flooded number one hold alive. The Italian crew promptly abandoned ship in the lifeboats. At least one account claims that the captain later fled, but was arrested, court-martialled and executed by the Germans.

In one account, the Italian hospital ship, the Arno, is accused of sailing straight through the scene, in which men were struggling in the water, supposedly on its way to the crew of a German boat which had been sunk nearby. Another version is that the Arno, which was based in nearby Navarino Bay, actually picked up injured survivors from the water. The destroyer that Dick referred to is perhaps more likely to have been the Italian torpedo boat, though another source also described it as a destroyer.

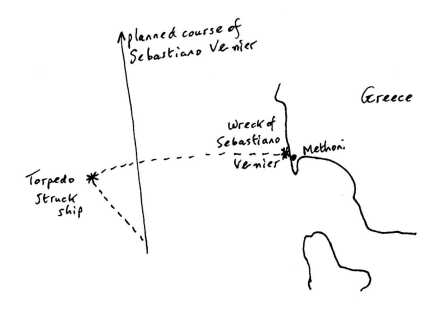

In rough sea and with the ship in danger of overturning, the successful approach to the coast is attributed to the sole German on board, [engineer or first mate] who had then taken charge. Flooding at the bow meant the ship was high in the water at the stern and the propellers were clear of the surface. The order to the crowd of men to go to the aft deck was to try to lower her at that end sufficiently to immerse the propellers and reach the coast and he managed eventually to accomplish this and then to reverse the ship over a submerged reef.

She was grounded adjacent to an old Venetian castle above a rocky beach at Methoni. Reports as to the distance from shore range from 30 to 90 metres. After a number of failed attempts to swim to shore by others, some of whom had drowned in the attempt, Lance Corporal Bernard Friedlander, a South African, managed to reach the beach with a rope tied round his waist, to which a cable was then attached and by which means many hundreds of prisoners reached land. Friedlander was awarded the George Cross for his achievement.

This photograph is attributed to an unknown Italian who was positioned next to Methoni Castle, while the Sebastiano Venier was floundering on the rocks with most of the POWs still on board. It is reproduced here with the permission of The Alexander Turnbull Library, Wellington, New Zealand, Collection Edge, Spence,
Ref: PA Coll-2242-1-2.

A South African Field Ambulance survivor, Newman Robinson, revisited Methoni in 1966 and filled in some more details by talking to the local people. "Some prisoners who succeeded in swimming ashore were quickly passed by the Greeks to a mustering point 10 kilometres east where they joined stragglers from the Allied campaign in Greece and were taken off by submarine." [p.38] If that was the case, they were very much the lucky ones when compared to the circumstances that those who remained behind found themselves in.

In June 1941 intelligence officers working at Bletchley Park had broken the code which enabled them to gain access to Italian Navy operations in the Mediterranean Sea. It is possible, therefore, that the intelligence services knew that the Sebastiano Venier was carrying POW's. Even so, it could not risk informing the submarine commander without risking a breech in the "Ultra" secret, as the capacity to break the code was referred to.

If the submarine's captain had been taken prisoner himself, theoretically he could have told his captors that he had been ordered to leave a particular ship alone, so he would not have been given that information at all. Other costly wartime events were effectively allowed to go ahead to keep intelligence secrets in this way, in other words, to act in favour of the greater good. This knowledge must have been a perplexing later addition to the known facts for the survivors of the tragedy.

When David told his dad about this revelation, how difficult it must have been for him to take. David recalls the conversation they had. "When I told Dad about this he went silent for a minute and was visibly quite upset and shocked. He knew nothing about it. He then remarked on how terrible it was that so many young people had died but then said, "I suppose they had to do it. It couldn't have been easy for the captain of the sub'," [that is, when he learnt later about the effects of his attack].

Sebastiano Venier, run aground near Methoni,
[reproduced with the permission of Methoni TV, Greece].

It is thought 320 Allied troops died in this event, as well as 12 Italian soldiers. At the National Memorial Arboretum in Staffordshire there is now a memorial plaque to the POWs lost at sea on the Sebastiano Venier.

The wreck of the ship was broken up in situ by the Greeks after the war. The keel remained, apparently visible during times of calm water, with sections of metal plate still to be found on the beach. In recent times, You Tube showed brief snippets of film made by snorkelers, around the remains at the scene.

"A sentry with a flickering lantern welcomed me and had the nerve to search me. He indicated a sodden group of half-clothed humanity standing beneath a shelf of rock. I joined this sorry crew, huddled against the rock, endeavouring to avoid the biting winds.

My clothes hung in sodden folds to my body and I realised the state I was in. My one desire was to get somewhere warm and dry. To my surprise my boots still clung round my neck and I pulled the sodden leather over my feet.

Some men were absolutely naked and blue with cold and exposure. They huddled in vain for shelter.

After a time, which seemed eternal we were marched up a winding path leading up a cliff face. A little walking brought us to a building, a barn affair. Inside the atmosphere was reeking with smoke and it was almost impossible to breathe. All night long I stood in this place and while the wood fires we had started lasted, I derived some cheer from their warmth. I tried to dry my clothes but it was impossible. Greek women came with raisins for us, but were driven away by the sentries. Hour after hour passed. The sodden floor made sleeping impossible.

At last came dawn and with the dawn, hope of another day. At approximately 10 o'clock our weary wait was over. Mentally, physically and morally worn out, we were led into the bright sunlight and lined up on the road. The warm sun striking friendly on my back was my only sympathiser. As if in sheer pity, the few black clouds dispersed, leaving patches of puffy white cloud, blue sky and bright sun.

There was an issue of a biscuit and a tin of bully, one biscuit per man and a tin of bully between two. Russell Yates and I sat on the roadside and with care and precision, divided the bully between us. Off came the biscuit wrapper and breakfast was served. I can still feel my teeth crunching contentedly on the hard dry biscuit and the saliva running in my mouth, even at the strange taste of Italian bully beef, the ingredients of which, I prefer not to know. Such was my first and last meal of that day. A repast fit for a king.

Having taken the edge off a permanent appetite and feeling a little stronger and in better spirits, I prepared for the road.

The green countryside was most refreshing compared with the eternal glare of the sun-drenched desert, and trying to forget the events of last night, I made the most of my walk.

Passing out of the village we could see the remains of our ship grounded in the harbour. I was safe. God had answered my fervent prayer and I felt certain He would be with me in the days to come. I knew now they would be blind days but worrying would not help.

As each mile went by my spirits rose. Walking leisurely through this Greek countryside, bathed in sunlight, fresh and green with many rains, its quaint villages glittering white on the hillsides, each with its little church. The fruit trees in their neat rows, the tall waving poplars: a riot of green trees and bushes glinting and laughing in the sunlight. No, I could not be miserable that morning, so forgetting my dejected companions and each of the miserable ill-clad guards with their rusty bayonets, I enjoyed these fleeting hours of happiness.

But eventually as each hour rattled by, the experience of the previous night, the sleep I had missed, told on me and the last of the seven miles found me weary but not miserable.

The town we arrived at was on the coast and it must have been one of the prettiest sights I have ever seen. The blue of the sun drenched Mediterranean, the gradual sweep of the bay with the sea rumbling and tumbling white over a golden shore. Mountains rising on either side of the bay, coloured a mystic purple, with houses gleaming white on the hills. There was a dried-up river we had to cross and a winding doubling road, which snaked down the mountainside. On our left a castle overlooked the sea, and as each step brought us nearer to this, our future prison, I drank in the glorious scenery around me. Finally I entered and the world was shut out. High walls encircled me and only a changing sky remained."

Italian occupying forces had been waiting on the shore at Methoni to recapture the surviving POWs. According to another piece of research, when it went dark most men were still aboard, where they stayed during the night. By the morning the weather had improved and more men came ashore on the lifeline. Others could now be brought ashore by small boats. The survivors were rounded up and taken to two warehouses in Methoni, where they too stayed overnight.

The operation to get the surviving men off the boat took place both on the day of the shipwreck and during the next morning. Dick's version implies that he got off on the 9th December and stayed in Methoni for just one night. Another detailed account of the event suggests that those leaving the boat the following day also had a night in the town. The POWs had then been marched to Pilos, on Navarino Bay, 12 kilometres to the north of

Methoni. It is likely, therefore, that they were taken there as two or more cohorts on consecutive days.

"Not much time was wasted. The men were pushed into long cells; thirty men per cell. A barrel of water was given to each cell, and a latrine bucket. The door had an iron grille. This was our only means of ventilation. But exhaustion made me oblivious to these cramped and confined conditions and all I wanted to do was sleep. Our happy home was barely 10 feet wide and about 25 feet long, so things were a bit crowded. By lying down interlocking our legs and all sleeping on the same side we managed to sleep pretty well. The sleeper on the right gave the orders to turn and we all turned together.

For three days we were confined to our cell, only being allowed out for check parade and half an hour in the morning air. Soon dysentery broke out and men no longer had control of themselves. Our hosts permitted us to carry helpless cases into a courtyard where there was a latrine where they had to fend for themselves, as best they could. My heart went out to these men and my position seemed paltry when compared to theirs.

After four days, vigilance relaxed and we were allowed to wander the courtyard. The weather being warm, I made the most of the fresh air, only returning to my prison at night, like cattle, we would be driven to where we would be padlocked for the night. I felt rather like a cow and expected to be milked any day.

Groups of Italian sailors without ships watched us from the high walls each day. It was possible to trade any remaining possessions. I swapped a leather tobacco pouch mother bought me on our last holiday together; I received seven Italian cigarettes. A disastrous price but I was dying for a smoke.

Rations came up at all hours of the day and were consumed immediately. We had one hot meal per day, which left you feeling hungrier than ever. Men gradually lost all respect and manners they had ever acquired in civilian life. If any food was left in the pots an orderly distribution was impossible. Discipline extended as far as each man receiving his ration and after that it was just a mad dash with the strongest to the pot and the weakest to the wall. These mad dashes with men fighting and scrambling for a spoonful of macaroni, even grovelling in the dust, sickened me and I was determined to starve rather than lower myself to their level.

The monotonous days passed. The dirt caked on me, in my hair, arms, legs and though it was horrible at first I grew accustomed to it. Each day my teeth got yellower and yellower and I ceased to care. There were rumours of moving and in the end they came true."

Built by the Turks in 1572 the castle at Pilos [or Pylos] had spent quite a lot of the intervening years up to the Second World War as a prison. The POWs were incarcerated in the dungeons of this castle. It had no doubt come as a bit of a surprise to the occupying Italian soldiers that they were going to have to look after around 1,500 new arrivals for a time.

As they were unexpected visitors it obviously made the task of looking after them a bit of an uphill struggle from the outset. Dick's intriguing explanation of how the food was distributed gives us a glimpse of his dignity in adversity and the fortitude he was determined to show. Even when things were this bad and folk around him had lost their self control, there were certain limits he was not prepared to stoop to. He was going to maintain his standards. That level of self belief would help him through the trials that no doubt still lay ahead.

"We were moved in lorries at 2 a.m. and after travelling all night drew up at a station and were put into trains. There followed a day's journey through Greece. On this trip I first caught a glimpse of ruthless Italian domination in this country. I saw a man smashed on the chest with the butt of a rifle. I saw children kicked and cattle potted at in the fields and many verbal displays of cruelty by this victorious Italian nation. I thought if we ever lose this war, I can expect no quarter from this barbarous swine.

We arrived at our destination at night and slept in the train. It was a bitterly cold night and the sentries lit large fires, which we could see but could not feel. A tantalising sight, reminding me of a hungry child pressing its nose against a shop window and knowing it will never eat

37

the cakes displayed.

The next day we were marched amply escorted – two sentries to three men – to an encampment eight miles from Patras on the Corinth Canal. Here we found men who had arrived three or four days before us.

Shortly this delightful little spot was to acquire the name of "dysentery acre" for obvious reasons. We were housed beneath Italian groundsheets with a little straw on the grounds for protection from the biting wind. Our position was becoming worse instead of better. The winter grew colder and to keep out this cold a well-worn Italian groundsheet was issued to each man. Many men were without boots and contracted frostbite. Dysentery, already a big factor, grew worse and during the 14 days I stayed there, latrines occupied more space than tents. Consequently more tents had to be crowded together to make room for these public conveniences. Men fell sick by the hundreds. There were over a thousand men cooped up in this enclosure. Hospital tents were erected and were always filled to capacity. Nights were spent huddled together trying to keep warm, and days tramping round the compound, trying to keep warm. I used to go to bed at 4.30 p.m. and sleep in starts until 10.00 a.m. when bread was issued. I would then light a small fire and huddle round it. I would toast my bread, eating it slowly, chewing it to a pulp. Not a morsel could I manage to save until night-time though I tried hard enough.

Lines of young oak trees, fresh and green, were torn down to mere stumps by naked hands. How we did it I do not know. Christmas Day came; the worst I have ever spent in my life. For a Christmas dinner we received a spoonful of raisins per man. I think there were ten raisins each. This and thin meat water, the chances of getting a piece of meat being negligible, comprised my ration for the day. Walking round the compound that night, thinking of last Christmas I could not suppress the tears from rolling down my face.

Perhaps the only relief was a hot shower on Christmas Eve. There were no towels but that made little difference. I was clean again and though my clothes were dirty that could not be helped.

The situation had reached a peak. The weather was vile and the ground reduced to a quagmire. Deaths were common and no one took much notice of the funeral processions, which were held daily. One just wondered when your turn would come, for you were certain to contract some disease sooner or later."

Patras is not, as Dick thought, on the Corinth Canal. It is further to the west and lies between the Gulf of Patras and the Gulf of Corinth. Dysentery Acre certainly achieved infamy and is mentioned in a number of memoirs. Overall, the evidence suggests a location at Akhaia, [now Achaia or Kato Achaia] though Robinson suggests a location further east. All agree that it was no more than a compound laid out with some Italian bivouac tents. Rain and snow had turned the surface into thick mud and it is claimed that the nearest clean water was obtained from a pump at a farm house several fields away.

Sparse rations and the fact that it was now a month since their capture, during which time they had had to put up with extreme hardship, means it is no surprise at all to read that death and disease were taking their toll. The contrast with the previous Christmas and the social life Dick had been enjoying before the war must have been hard to bear. That he allowed himself a moment of emotion seems so restrained. I can't help feeling that by that point there would be some men who must have been in a far worse psychological state than he was.

> "Finally after sixteen days of misery and hunger, we were bundled into lorries and taken to Patras, a port near the Corinth Canal. We arrived at night and a promised hot meal never materialised.
>
> It is difficult to describe our new home. It housed a thousand men and consisted of a warehouse with three-tier racks, about 8 feet in width stretching up and down, one each side and two in the middle. There were two of these bungalows separated by a courtyard with a tap in it. Half this courtyard was occupied by the cookhouse. Outside the courtyard beyond a high wall was a wired compound, where latrines were dug. The warehouses were side on to the sea front. Exercise was impossible as your limits were up and down the gangways and in the small courtyard. The main source of amusement consisted of waiting for the bread to arrive in the morning and standing watching the meal cooking. The scale of rations was slightly better but as I had lost all my excess fat and my bones were poking through my skin and my ribs showing, I was always hungry.
>
> I caught my first louse at Dysentery Acre, the sight of which was revolting. But in Patras, the bungalows seethed with them and I grew accustomed to the blood sucking pest. At first I could feel them biting me but as the days passed they ceased to worry me. I deloused my shirt and vest three times per day and if I failed to catch 300 at a sitting I was very lucky. The lice teemed and crawled. We wallowed in our filth, unshaven, bitter, hopeless. Each day dragged on. Men's minds cracked and they were carried gibbering away. January passed. February dawdled by, but the boat seemed further away. We watched them draw into Patras harbour and draw out again. Stories of sunny Italy were encouraging and we longed to be out there.
>
> I broke out in sores all over my legs. They were ugly things. A dab of iodine every two days was the only treatment. I kept walking as much as possible to keep the blood running. I also developed whitlows on my

fingers. All my efforts to keep cheerful failed and I sank into hopeless despair. Then I developed a swelling on my neck. I didn't know what it was but I could not eat no matter how hungry I was. I tried soaking my bread and managed to swallow a little over a period of time. My throat was daily painted with iodine.

It was possible to trade a little with the Greeks through the Italians. The Greeks were in a very sorry state and were not allowed rations. They existed mainly on raisin pasties. These were manufactured simply by moulding raisins together into little cakes, covering them with caraway seeds and placing them in an oven for a few minutes. For a loaf of bread you could get fifteen of these pasties. To us, devoid of any sweetness, these were a god send and I am convinced saved many men's lives. Fifteen pasties were also much more satisfying than a loaf of bread. So everyday I traded one of my small loaves. Cigarettes were also obtainable for bread, but this was a hard sacrifice. For two pasties you could get three cigarettes and I often traded in this fashion. By trading and re-trading I could buy back my original loaf and also have cigarettes and pasties into the bargain. This was a lengthy process but while I was fit it helped to occupy my time.

As time drew on I could hardly walk. Each day seemed darker and more hopeless. Singapore had capitulated and our war situation was rather precarious."

After a painful fortnight or so at Akhaia, Dick and his companions finally reached Patras, the embarkation port for Bari, in Italy. They were there for about five weeks, held in the warehouses, which suggests that they were actually in, or at least on the edge of, the town itself. Little appears to have been reported about this latest transit camp.

As Dick's condition clearly continued to deteriorate, he still managed to build a bit of purpose into his day, by conducting some entrepreneurial business activity in the midst of all the squalor. This would surely give him a slight satisfaction, to realise that even here, if he could keep his head together, he could use his ingenuity to make a small improvement in his lot. It made me smile to read it. I was impressed by his ingenuity.

"About the beginning of March we moved down to the boat. I was helped down by some friends and lain in the hold on a mattress. Food on this ship was much better and I was able to eat a little. For counts, men were filed up on deck and counted back into the hold. I, being unable to walk, remained below with the sick.

Our main reason for moving was the outbreak of meningitis in the bungalows. There were about seven deaths and many men were put into isolation. The Italians got pretty panicky over this and even supplied us with gargle.

I breathed a sigh of relief. At last I was on a boat and though I felt sick in the body and spirit, to be on a boat and going somewhere added a little hope to my position.

Our boat drew over into the bay and remained there three days, more of an isolation ship. Below me there was a chap with pneumonia and during one of the counts, they brought down an Italian doctor to see him. No interpreter came with the doctor and by mistake he saw me. Looking at my throat for the first time with care, he showed great concern and informed me that on arrival in Italy, he would place me in hospital. But that afternoon I was placed in a picket boat and taken ashore. We passed a Red Cross ship and my weary mind worked overtime, thinking that I should travel to Italy aboard her.

There were five of us altogether and we were taken through Patras and into Patras Hospital. As a hospital it stank, but considering the insanitary conditions I had grown accustomed to, it was an absolute heaven.

I discarded my disreputable clothes, put on pyjamas and sank with relief beneath the sheets for a while content.

Thin rice was served at 5 p.m. and a glass of milk. I slept deeply until morning when I woke to the sound of birds: a cup of ersatz coffee stood at my elbow.

The three diets served at this hospital were;
1. Milk – this consisted of two glasses of milk per day.
2. Light diet – Milk twice a day, thin rice twice a day [occasionally half a bread loaf.]
3. Full diet – The usual Italian stew twice a day, 400 grams of bread, a spoonful of jam, a small piece of meat, veg or beans and fruit.

Food did not concern me for the first week and I could not even drink my milk. I became steadily worse instead of better. At times I felt it was useless to carry on, hanging onto life which was so brimful of suffering. But I had other moods. The image of my mother; all she had sacrificed for me and the possibility that Dorothy and I should feel the same towards each other, kept me going. The realisation that I must fight now so that I would realise the benefits that must lie somewhere in the future. Memories of the past and the conviction that life was still worthwhile, that this was only a cruel phase and it would pass, kept me from sinking into oblivion.

I have faint memories of injections, of being turned over and stabbed, and then turned back again to continue my semiconscious existence. I could see my bed mates but it did not matter. Sounds outside had no effect. I seemed to float about not knowing anything, but numb. I remember somebody coming to dress my wounds and sores. He was very gentle, removing the filthy bandages. My fingers and legs were green and crawling with lice.

Slowly but surely fighting against a force which was pressing against my brain, the fever left me and my eyes saw clearly again. I tried to turn my head but a twinge told me my neck was still the same. I raised my hand and touched it. The swelling seemed very large.

A few days later, very weak, I was helped down to the operating theatre, shuffling down the corridors in my rather small pyjamas. A doctor examined me and asked a few questions. I was then placed on an operating table. Two men pinned me down at my feet and head and a nurse grasped my hand. There was something calming about that girl's hand. Then a pause, a flash of a surgical knife, a blinding pain, blood spurting as the abscess was contacted and broken. The blood trickled warm down my neck. It was swabbed up with masses of cotton wool. Now there was no more pain, so I relaxed, dazed and breathing hard. Somebody was cutting a piece of rubber tubing. This cut length was inserted in my neck. Just a few minutes more while they bandaged me and then a dizzy walk, back to my bed where I slept for hours.

The days passed ever so slowly. I could walk unattended to have my wound dressed and grew to enjoy these respites from the ward. We had to go to the far end of the hospital across a courtyard. I must have struck a pathetic figure shuffling across to the dressing station. Once a Greek nurse shyly walked up to me and gave me a fig. Such a small gift but it made me feel I had struck a friend in this unfriendly place. The Greek dresser was sympathetic but guarded in his sympathy.

Our rations, if they had not been filched at their source, were quite good but unfortunately the Italian orderlies would use our rations to pay for their washing and their nights out. Most women in Greece sold themselves for food. I do not blame them, for they were starving. Rice and macaroni were put aside and we were left with the gypo [mainly water]. Meat was halved and omelettes cut into three.

One day we complained to the doctor and the food improved considerably. During our convalescence George O'Neil, a South African who I became friendly with, often rifled the orderly's cupboard at night when he was out, usually with success. One night Mario, that was the orderly's name, turned us all out of bed endeavouring to find a large loaf which was not the general hospital issue. We spent an exciting hour but the loaf was never found. There was a Cypriot who amused us by jumping on his bed demanding the jam issue. His wealth of black hair was cut off one day. He looked quite perturbed.

But apart from these slight relaxations the boredom of the place was nerve racking. George, the Cypriot, a New Zealander and I played Ludo with a home made set. Scotty, another Englishman, was injected day after day without sympathy until he was unable to lie down on his back.

One guard from the Carabiniere watched over us and occasionally gave us cigarettes. One in particular sang us songs in a rich baritone voice. He had travelled to England and had broadcast over our radio. I shall remember the joy he brought into our lives. One night after missing him for about three days, he brought us presents of cigarettes and cake and sang late into the night. But he went away shortly afterwards and we never saw him again.

About the end of March George and I were moved to a so-called convalescent camp in the hills. The meningitis isolation patients were isolated here, waiting for the boat. We waited too, spending our time sitting in the sun which had grown quite warm. Lack of food made you dizzy if you stayed out too long.

*My sole possessions were a shirt, a torn battle-dress blouse and a New Zealand overcoat. The days passed flogging our bread for pasties; waiting on each meal; keeping down the lice which fortunately were not so numerous; laughing and finding our plight even humorous at times; sitting with minds sometimes blank and sometimes dreaming; sweating life and death on the possibility of getting any buckshee *skilly. [*watery stew.]*

In April we moved. There were thirty-six of us altogether and as a gesture bread and bully were issued. Small lorries took us down to the quayside. The boat was different from anything we had been accustomed to since capture. We had third class accommodation; a bed with real springs in it. The food was excellent and the sailors sympathetic. We messed with the Italian sailors and what they did not eat, they brought down to us. They were gala days and for the first time I was bloated and unable to eat any more. But the trip was an anxious one and we had a haunting fear that we might have to swim for it again."

Dick had been held in four different locations in Patras over a period of between three and four months at the beginning of 1942, firstly the transit camp then the isolation ship and from there to the hospital. Finally, it was back out of town and into the hills for a period of convalescence.

Before the development of a modern teaching hospital, the main hospital in Patras was Saint Andreas [now Agios Andreas], but there were other smaller private hospitals, including a military one which could have been used at that time. Both German and Italian troops were stationed in the city during the occupation. Patras remains the main ferry port for crossings of the Adriatic, serving various locations in Italy today, including Brindisi and Bari.

"We landed at Bari on a Sunday, immediately coming onto army rations which was vastly different from the navy. Bari camp was reached on Monday night. It was bitterly cold standing outside the office waiting to be searched and I was numb and parched when we were shown behind the wire.

That night I tasted English tea for the first time since 29th November. There was no milk or sugar but it tasted good. I picked up Maple leaf tins, cheese cartons, bully labels of various makes. Surely this was too good to be true. I remembered the forgotten and much doubted Red Cross Parcels. Tomorrow was issue day, one parcel between four men. I spent a restless sleepless night thinking of the joy tomorrow would bring. It rained heavily that night and as is customary with Italian barracks the roof leaked. As we were sleeping on the floor our blanket and palliases suffered...

Our parcel materialised as promised. With triumph I carried the clean new box with its present contents back to my three companions. My hand shook too much to split this parcel satisfactorily and I left it to George. With infinite care each tin was split between four, and with eager eyes, wide and wondering, we watched. Not one minute portion could afford to be wasted. That night was a gala night and by morning my quarter parcel was just a pleasant and tantalising memory.

At Bari, we were forced to work mornings and afternoons. The days were warm and provided there was no "El Capitano" about not a great deal was done. But the sentries were scared stiff of this taskmaster. When he was about, standing on his favourite perch, silent, critical, we were driven with our wheelbarrows at the point of a rusty bayonet.

But the work, though it was at times irksome, occupied the time and brought us sound sleep at night. It also helped to keep my mind off food and evenings with their spelling B's and stump speeches were quite pleasant. The lice problem was not so bad and I even reduced my searches to once every two days. It was also possible to have a shave once a week, which was very good. During the first week I slept on the floor, but later, officers were moved to another camp and I managed to secure one of the camp beds.

Our life carried on, the reluctant call to work morning and afternoon, chatting with the Italian sentries in our broken Italian. The more talk, the less work. Picking your working party, looking out for El Capitano. The groans and protests when "Via Via" was screeched and bawled at us: the contempt we felt for these ill-clad temperamental swine. The longing to be free and whether working or otherwise, the knowledge that you were always being watched and that there was always, two feet, a faded blue uniform and a bayonet trotting behind.

Easter 1942 was one of the most enjoyable days. A holiday was granted. Red Cross parcels were issued one between two. This issue was a great and glorious step in our PoW life. So much good food had never come our way for months. With pent up excitement I waited for mine and with sheer joy clutched the clean Canadian box. If there was a happier man in the world then he must have been very happy. All afternoon we made trifles, decorating them with Happy Easter and other such greeting and trying to recapture slightly the feeling of joy and good fellowship on such a day as Easter. At night-time the tea arrived and we devoured our rich concoctions. I am pleased to say I felt heartily sick. Others were sick. By Monday very little of my half a parcel remained but I had enjoyed it and succeeded in banishing for a day that strange unexplainable feeling which pervades every minute of this PoW life in its early stages, until one learns to be patient and grows accustomed to it.

But Easter passed and though parcels were issued one between four at irregular intervals, these passed also and there were no more. Our thoughts wandered to that permanent camp and we longed to be there. We still thought there were better places but were yet to learn the Bari Camp was the best we should strike in Italy.

One morning a Roman Catholic Padre arrived at the camp with a story full of colour: parcels, one whole parcel per week, comfortable sleeping quarters, in fact a Butlins holiday camp into which we would soon be transferred. Our camp fairly buzzed with expectancy and we longed for the day that we should move."

Bari Campo 75, referred to as Torre Tresca in a list of former Italian POW camps, is represented today by a named radial road, Strada Torre Tresca, which leads out of the city to the south, two miles from the centre and on towards the current outer ring road, an industrial estate and the football stadium.

A contemporary New Zealander's wartime account suggests that had Dick been there even a few months earlier, conditions might have been even worse. He comments on the overcrowding and the particularly unpleasant camp commandant, but suggests that as the transit camp became more permanent, there was a reduction in the numbers of POWs, better food and improved sanitation by the spring of 1942.

"At last we moved, marching three miles into Bari. We paraded through

streets, the civilians agape at this weird collection of human beings, ill clad, their scanty possessions under their arms or in dirty haversacks. The journey was tiring and the stupid staring eyes of the Italians annoyed me considerably and I boarded the train glad to be away from their gaze.

We arrived at Gravina Camp late at night and after a march across a field, entering Prisoner of War Camp 65, my home for 16 months.

16 months of prison life, which started from nothing and by a series of lucky breaks I was able to build up, a certain comfortable civilisation, which I would be sorry to leave. Here eventually I had enough to eat and was able to secure many things, which were denied to other prisoners. This camp was in a desolate part of Southern Italy between Tutarama and Gravina. There were only three bungalows when we first arrived with a complement of eight hundred men. Each bungalow was split into five sections with twenty-four double beds per bay.

The men in this camp were in a sorry state. Their rations consisted of a handful of soggy bread, said to weigh 250 grams, a small cube of cheese and a hot watery meal at night. The macaroni and rice content could often be counted in the bottom of the Dixie. At midday "greenwater" was served. This consisted of dandelion leaves and other roots boiled. Occasionally there was a little cabbage or pea content. It was the worst tasting concoction you could imagine. Vegetable stalks, declared unfit for human consumption, were ravenously devoured by everyone. Meat days occurred twice per week, usually on a Saturday and Sunday. On these days there was no cheese issue. Instead a small portion of lifeless over-boiled meat was issued. The only well-fed men in the camp were the cooks and they controlled the camp.

The first issue of Red Cross parcels took three weeks and men were tormented waiting for the day. There was no official method of issue. Some days they would issue a hundred and the next day none at all.

Malnutrition swept the camp and men's bodies were mere skeletons. Thighs and legs were scarcely the thickness of a man's arm. Weak and listless, they dragged themselves about the camp and would faint on parade. This permanent craving for food was made worse for there was nothing to do but wait for each night to pass and each day to bring on bed time again. Ceaseless boredom and hunger played on men's minds.

CPC [Chief Petty Officer] Anscombe was the first man to try and get some form of organisation in the camp, though he had many difficulties to encounter. The Italian authorities would give us nothing. Some prisoners were stubborn men, who would not help themselves or help other people. They wallowed in their own self-pity and sentiment and would not wash or at least try to keep themselves clean.

The spasmodic issue of Red Cross parcels helped considerably and must have saved many lives.

I could devote page after page to the serious lice situation, bad sanitation, no hospital facilities or equipment, no anti-malarial treatment, a disease which swept through the camp, overcrowding in the huts, slush and mud wet days, the lack of water, but I shall not do so. The conditions were the worst you could imagine and it was a full year before they improved.

At one stage the minds of the men were just animal, looking and acting like hungry wolves cooking and eating grass; coffee grouts; searching through garbage piles. It was impossible to believe that conditions could make men act like this. They obeyed the dictates of their stomachs and providing that was full, which never was, they were happy.

For any improvements to the camp we must thank the Red Cross, and to volunteer working parties, which men dragged themselves out to. For a day's work they received an extra loaf* of bread and macaroni. [*An Italian loaf was the size of a small dinner roll but of a denser texture.]

Since being captured my full issue of clothing from the enemy included a shirt and two pairs of Italian underpants. Any other clothes came from the Red Cross and from my personal parcels. The food they gave me was enough to keep one in the state I have mentioned and any other came from the Red Cross and without that I should be lost.

But in the end PG 65 was fit to live in. The change came gradually with the improvement of Red Cross parcels supplies, and when I left I was sorry, for I had an excellent job cooking and catering for some medical officers and padres, who lived in the infirmary. My mind was fully occupied and I worked hard. At first my job was filled with many difficulties for I could not get co-operation from either the Italians or our own men as regards cooking facilities but by persuasion and at times force, changes took place and in the end my job was easy."

The modern aerial photograph of the road between Altamura and Gravina, two towns separated by only a short distance of about eight miles, shows clearly where this camp must surely have been located. Two huts remain in situ, but the outlines are there for a whole settlement, with the grid iron pattern of paths between them still visible. Gravina is in the Province of Bari, so Dick's day long journey to reach it, with treks at both ends of the event, really only took him about 40 miles inland.

Dick never had an opportunity to investigate Google Earth and its window on the world. It might have been possible for him to zoom in on his own past to a literally frightening degree. Even where the landscape has changed, as in the case of the Gravina camp, there are still glaring graphic reminders in the aerial photographs which might have made for extremely uncomfortable viewing. Much better that he stuck with his memories, his written notes and the detailed and moving account that they led to.

Gravina Camp 65, with 8,000 inmates and sitting on a ridge surrounded by farmland growing wheat, did not get a good press. It was described as, "rivalling Bari as a bad camp" and having, "an atmosphere of overbearing truculence and petty restrictions." There was a meningitis outbreak there too, in early 1942, though deaths amongst prisoners attributed to this disease may actually have been caused by malnutrition and starvation, according to other reports. Even the corrupt camp commandant gets a mention elsewhere, for selling on clothes, boots and food intended for the POWs.

Newman Robinson was also in this camp and he put it like this, "Food became absurdly, monstrously, important. It became an obsession with all of us. We thought about nothing else all day; dreamed about it at night…." [p. 52.]

But, there was also a kind of devolution set up here in which each section was organised by a British or South African Regimental Sergeant Major, who was allowed to appoint his own police, cooks, barbers, wood choppers etc. Those employed in this way, including Dick, it seems, stood to gain double rations as a result. Did that lead to a lot of resentment from those not chosen? Would the chosen few care?

"Fermo: PoW Camp 70. Moved north to this camp in June 1943 after

the Ities packed in – 8th September 1943.

Our conversations on this subject have often resulted in long discussions, sometimes far into the night. Many poems have been written with this question as inspiration. All the while, as prisoners of war, we watched, waited, hoped and dreamed that one day it would come true.

Sept. 8th 1943, we learned that the Italians had capitulated. On that memorable night I was lying in Leo Mundy's tent listening to an impromptu band concert, a few of the band busking for their own amusement. Strange how I enjoyed these efforts so much better than the organised band concert.

The evening was passing favourably and there did not seem to be any dragging between teatime and bedtime. There was the usual conversation around the latest advance of our troops in Reggio Calabria, the usual claims about stupendous advances. We wished them success but still felt that we were miles away and rather remote. Liberation seemed so far away and we were so impatient.

Jack Day had been out for a walk and among his stories, he told us that on asking the sentry when the war would end, he was informed it had ended. This story was received with a smile. Later that evening the Italian sentries were heard shouting and screaming with joy. Our hearts sank. Must be bad news.

The band played on. A rustling rumour commenced to float through our midst and in the dimming light Frank Lazzari told us the news we had been waiting for, but not expecting so soon, for so long. "Do not be alarmed," he said "but the Italians have capitulated." With these words softly spoken in my ear, everything seemed to swim. I could not hear the band. I went first hot then clammy. My heart pounded against my ribs and for a moment I could not realise the significance of Frank's words. The tension inside me rose higher and higher until I thought my head would burst. Then my head went clear again and I lay back, dazed and a little bewildered. The band played "God Save The King." "Come on Leo," I shouted, "Let's see if it's true." Out we went into the starlit night, eager, wondering and still a little doubtful.

But there was no doubt of its truth. Announcements had been made on the loudspeakers. We had been asked to remain calm. Everybody was cheering. The all clear was sounded, more cheering and "God Save The King" was played again. Still cheering and jubilation at the wonderful turn in fate. Leo and I went up to see Captain Milburn. There were crowds, slapping of backs, hatred of the Italians lost, jolly good fellows all round, drunk in the new hope which flowed through us. We fought our way out of the crowd and together, almost alone, walked round the compound, a thousand teeming questions crowding our brains. Behind us the cheering was still there, the band playing patriotic songs, a velvet night of scintillating stars our first night of peace. We were a little dazed and could not appreciate the significance of our position. There seemed so many obstacles to conquer before we were out of danger and back with our own people. But we were so relieved that at least one, and the major obstacle, had been passed. A brew was indicated. We returned to see Bob Everett and Tom Summerfield. There was a brew waiting. It had been made before the Armistice and was without sugar. I added the necessary sweetener. So the night passed. The cheering died down, the crowds went to bed, the band dispersed and save for the many flickering fires making celebrating brews, quiet descended once more.

Morning dawned and to celebrate this victory morn, we had a rather longer breakfast than usual. Though we were still behind the wire, the world seemed a brighter, cheerier place. Leo and I went to a Thanksgiving Service and idled the morning, talking and discussing the future.

Bathing parades were arranged and we went down to a nearby river where we attempted to swim in scarcely three feet of water. It was pleasant sitting on the banks of the river. I found my reactions quite normal. There was no desire to plunder the countryside, get drunk or find myself a woman. I was content to wander about the pleasant country lanes, glad to be away from that well pounded prison walk on the inside of the perimeter of the camp. There was peace there and we were able to tear ourselves apart from the seething humanity we had lived with for so long. The bottom gate of the camp was open continually and men streamed through paying no attention to dress. Perhaps, after two years spent in all manner of dress makes it difficult for men to realise that even in a country district, underpants are not the right kind of dress or hiking gear. A certain amount of crops were damaged and pillaged. Some of us got very drunk. For the actions of the few, many had to suffer. But the damage was low in my opinion and Colonel Papa showed a narrow-minded point of view. Nearly all the grapes round here are of a very poor quality, unpruned and unmarketable.

I was convinced that when the first lust for fruit had passed and the desire for alcohol sickened us, the behaviour of the men would be no worse than is expected in an ordinary barracks.

Desertion was easy. A man could pack his bag and openly walk out of the camp. There was a complete lack of discipline and lead from our HQ, and men were left to their own devices. But at the same time, told, that leaving the camp meant desertion and action would be taken against offenders.

Our constant fear was German intervention, but we were lulled with stories of Italian divisions protecting us should the Germans come this way. This did not hearten me for the best Italians cannot fight, so I am sure the dregs of Italy will not fight either. The country to my mind was a no man's land. If our forces arrive OK but if the Germans came all would be up.

Discipline seemed to get worse instead of better and nobody seemed to have the guts to dictate. Men wandered through the back gate and stayed out a couple of days. Returning only to fetch more vests and pants with which to trade.

Colonel Papa decided that we were robbing the poor Italian peasants, so put his sentries on the gate and the situation returned to pre-peace stage. The following day, walks were arranged in parties of four. On the same day Italians up to the rank of sergeant were paid off and by night time there was not a sentry to be seen.

This particular day John Ingham, John Thomson, Tom Summerfield, Jack Nicholls, Jim Hacket and myself went for a walk. We enjoyed a glorious tramp, way over the hills in a southward direction, taking our fill of apples, figs and grapes. The countryside from each rising hill was captivating. We swapped some socks and soap for bread, returning tired to camp at 6.30 p.m. That evening we strolled as far as a nearby granary and talked for some time to the manager, who showed us a map of Italy.

Feeling in the camp that night was high. The men were crying out for a leader and everyone was in two minds whether to go or not. At a meeting that night it was decided that it was inadvisable to leave camp and we were strongly advised to stay.

The following day Leo and I took a ramble over the hills to the north. Tramping beneath the hot sun was sweating work but at two o'clock we arrived at a little farmhouse about 5 kilometres away. Tom had given me a pair of underpants to trade, for which I got 8 eggs and 2 kilos of potatoes. Leo did likewise with a shirt. We asked if we might stay to lunch. We were invited into the farmhouse consisting of bare whitewashed walls and stone floor. In one corner stood a rough bench and there was also a narrow table and a couple of chests. On one side of the room was an open fireplace. A witch's cauldron bubbled with hot *water over its meagre flames.*

Our lunch was partaken with the family and consisted of macaroni stew, containing a few tomatoes, olive oil and potatoes. A hunk of bread was given to each of us. Leo and I had a bottle of wine between us. It seemed impossible that human beings could exist on macaroni, dry bread and wine. They had no boots or socks and their clothes were little better than rags. We as prisoners of war have everything to look forward to. They have nothing. I enjoyed this brief insight into the lives of the peasant families. On the return we had a swim. A short walk at night completed a perfect day and we returned to camp eating grapes.

After parade on the 18th September 1943, the camp was quietly taken over by the Germans."

Fermo 70 was a disused, flax processing factory, with large concrete warehouses, west of Porto St Giorgio and only a few miles from the Adriatic Coast. It was employed again after 1945, firstly holding displaced Croatians and later reverting to its former use, but this time making leather products.

Dick does not describe what must have been a lengthy journey northwards, up the length of the "leg" of mainland Italy to Fermo, that he made in June 1943. During his time in this camp, he became part of the production team of a hand written newspaper, the "Seventy Times," which was then posted on a wall. In drag, he also played Elizabeth Imbrie, in the camp production [doubly appropriate, of course] of "The Philadelphia Story."

Finding purpose in the face of boredom, publicly demonstrating one's own self worth, summoning the self discipline and effort required to make a contribution when physically undernourished and revelling in the sheer enjoyment that comes from involvement, must have been critical morale boosters at times of such adversity. It shows character and personality to get stuck into such positive use of time behind the wire. It does not surprise me at all that Dick was in the frame for both.

American, British and Commonwealth troops invaded Sicily on 10th July 1943. After battles that were very costly on both sides, the Germans retreated to mainland Italy and were pursued north by the Allies. On the 8th September an armistice was announced, an initially secret deal having been made with Britain and America, which effectively meant that Italy had surrendered.

By the time this had been announced, a new Italian government was already in place and Mussolini had been imprisoned. The occupying Germans quickly disarmed the Italians in the areas they controlled, which was still most of the country. Hitler decided to continue to defend Italy as far south [and as far away from Germany itself] as was possible.

"They were so convinced that they couldn't move us that it came as a

shock when orders came through that we were moving. They, who thought the Germans were too occupied in moving themselves, found their organisation was strong enough to move us too.

At 3 p.m. on the 23rd September that familiar call "Group Commanders" by which the "griff" [news] comes, good or bad, blew loud and clear, and at the double. Ten minutes later the truth was learnt, "move at 4 p.m" and the camp was in uproar. It's strange how, instead of an atmosphere of misery pervading the air, the feeling is one of amusement. Nothing can shake us really and be the news good or bad, we take it in our stride. Our fate was sealed. No use crying over spilt milk and there had been some spilling this time. We packed and after a brew with Leo, waited to move off. This took some time and was spent chatting.

Eventually, after much delay, our party moved off. Going out of the Gate, a Red Cross parcel and ten cigarettes was given to each man.

We were packed into cattle trucks, fifty men per truck. It's surprising how many men can squeeze into these things. Arriving at Porto St Georgio, we boarded trucks on the main line.

There were forty men allotted to each truck. The doors were locked all the way. We were supplied with a dixie of water; some cheese and three days' bread ration. We spent four days in this confined space. Journeys of this kind are a rare experience, which shatters all illusions as what your captors can do and what you can do as a prisoner of war. Sleeping accommodation consisted of stretching oneself on the floor as best you could. In the early hours of the morning, I woke stiff, cold and unrefreshed, after a troubled sleep. Each day was insufferably long, and our beards grew longer. We did not talk much. Mile after mile raced beneath us, taking us nearer to Germany. A hole in the floorboards served as a latrine. We occasionally clambered up and looked out of the grills, which were at each corner of our moving prison.

On the second day we were allowed out to relieve ourselves: a quarter of an hour's freedom, a few rushed words with friends in other trucks, grins through dirty faces, sparks of humour through our gloom and then back to our trucks. The doors slammed once more. The bolts slid home and we were left for another two days. Occasionally we ate, crouched over our bread, our knives sticky with butter and jam, our plates dirty from previous meals. Our tempers grew a little raw but we held ourselves. Four long days confined and then fresh air, and a little more freedom again and this experience recedes into a memory.

We arrived at Stalag IVB via a camp in a place called Jacobsthal, one of the most God forsaken places I have ever been to. It was rumoured to be a medical experimental camp."

Dick sensed correctly that there was a particularly unpleasant atmosphere at Jacobsthal. Stalag IVB Zeithain was inaugurated in April 1941 in the grounds of a military training establishment, alongside Jacobsthal railway station. It was made a branch camp of Stalag IVB in September 1942 and the following February it was converted to become POW Reserve Hospital Zeithain. Its official purpose was to house Soviet POWs who were too ill to work. In reality, it was a death camp for sick Soviet prisoners, who were dying at rates of between 10 and 25 per day, largely from typhoid and tuberculosis. British POWs were held there briefly in 1943 simply because when they arrived, there was no room for them immediately at Stalag IVB.

> *"Stalag IVB was a large camp, housing many nationalities, including Russians, who were very badly treated. By this time we were hardened prisoners of war, used to being counted, searched, stood outside for hours on end. We could switch off to all these inconveniences. It was all part of our day. Huts holding several hundred men, with three tier continuous bunks, were not bad. They had tables and benches at one end and a stove for cooking on. Our combine, Tom Summerfield, Bob Everett, Leo Mundy and myself shared everything and though the strains of incarceration caused tension, we were of infinite help to each other. We created our own civilisation behind the wire. I was interested in the theatre with Leo who produced many shows and radio plays. We would visit a hut at night, erect a screen to hide us and then enact a play. They were very popular.*"

Dick, in drag, during one of Stalag IVB's musical productions.

> *"I was also on the camp newspaper as a reporter. I taught myself shorthand, though why, goodness knows.*

Food was a portion of black bread and boiled potatoes once a day. Provided there was a reasonable supply of Red Cross Parcels we could organise a passable and sustaining diet but if these failed, as they did from time to time, life was a bit thin and we got even thinner. The Germans did not puncture the tins, as the Italians did, so we always tried to save for lean times. Musical instruments could be bought off Germans for cigarettes. So by charging cigarettes to see plays and shows we were able to buy musical instruments and also hire costumes and props.

The German officers were keen on the theatre and would be invited to the first night. In a camp of many thousands we had some wonderful musicians of many nationalities and at this time I first took an interest in classical music.

There was an order issued that all PoWs [Prisoners of War] would salute German Non-Commissioned Officers when walking down the main camp Road. This was repugnant to us so a party was arranged to march down the road without wearing hats. They of course passed a German N.C.O., failed to salute, were arrested and brought before the Commandant. It was explained to him that, in the British army it was an insult to salute an officer when not wearing a hat. He pondered for a little time and then dismissed the case without punishment. The order was never enforced again."

In January 1995, Dick added the passage above, about his time at Stalag IVB, Muhlberg-on-Elbe, in order to complete his story.

"On the night of June 21st 1944 Joe Brown was shot by a German Lance Corporal whilst crawling through the wire between D compound and the Russian Pioneer Park. The German came from behind a building and without warning shot him between the eyes. He died about an hour later. He was supposed to be going after strawberries.

Friday 13th April 1945. The day of freedom is very close. A sudden dash by our forces on the other side of the Elbe might bring us the freedom we have all been longing for these long years. Three and a half years have passed since that memorable day when we were over-run south of Tobruk on the 29th November 1941.

A prisoner's life has its ups and downs but taken as a whole, it is filled more with disappointments than pleasant surprises. We rely exclusively upon the Red Cross for all forms of comfort and should this fine institution fail us, as it has done from time to time, then life becomes more monotonous than ever. Without it, the craving of our stomachs becomes almost unbearable, for rations from detaining powers are inadequate to the extreme. The detaining powers barely fulfil their obligations for rations. Their bare ration of food was sufficient only to keep you alive and should one fall sick, everything is left to luck. Without the Red Cross, malnutrition becomes rife, men's tempers are unbearable and worse still sickness can hardly be counteracted, should it break out to any extent.

So Red Cross permitting, some times have been better than others and on occasion, I have even had some good fun, especially during the latter days at PG65 and last summer, swimming in that filthy pool across by the football pitch in Stalag IVB. Winters are a dread with their slush, mud and intense cold. Food always seems so short during this period and we breathe sighs of relief when the sun breaks through the sky suffusing its gentle warmth through our thin frames.

All my activities have been more or less forced and total immersion in any job has been very difficult. I have found that my eye has always been on the clock no matter how hard I have tried to resist the temptation.

I have tried to abide by a few rules, which I summarise as follows,
1. Keep as clean as possible.
2. Keep your temper; tolerate the violent outburst of your fellows remembering that they too are suffering the same nervous strain as yourself.
3. Do not talk or think about food.
4. When the parcels are in, do a little PT to keep fit.

These simple precautions have been hard to abide by and I know that I have on many occasions gone right off the rails. It has been comforting to know that I have never known how long I would be a prisoner. Always another six months to go has been my policy and that has stretched out to three and a half years. I am sure that it may be tomorrow or the next day and at the most a couple of weeks before I am on the other side of the wire. These last days are by no means easy because of the stubborn and fanatical resistance of Germany.

Each day the area of our camp becomes more and more the centre of activity as the Anglo-American forces press onward towards the River Elbe, threatening Dresden, Leipzig and Chemnitz. We are even past the rumour stage and excitement grows tenser by the day. We are too impatient really, expecting them here far too soon and expressing annoyance should the advances not meet with our expectations. Ears press to the news bulletins each night and we anxiously wonder when will they jump the last river.

Aerial activity increases daily – Lockheed Lightnings and Thunderbolts, flash and scream down in the bright sunlight to deliver their concentrated steel pills on railway sidings, trucks, roads and numerous insignificant targets in the vicinity, even to groups of soldiers passing along the roads. The night re-echoes with the drone of heavy bombers, roaring overhead to Berlin and other targets and the bungalows, we inhabit, shake with the explosions of heavy calibre bombs.

So our life grows tenser and I am not by a long chalk out of the wood. Who knows what tomorrow may bring? So far the camp has been untouched and I am sure that our planes know that this is a prison camp and I am convinced that no direct attacks will be made upon us, by this constant Hendon air display, which fills our ears throughout the day. There is, of course, the possibility of being moved but this is remote in my opinion. For where are we going to move to? Still one never knows what is going to happen and I only hope something happens in the next few days to clarify our rather awkward predicament.

Today the internal administration of the camp was taken over by Lt Jessop, by order of the Germans and we were told that the guards round about were merely there to keep law and order. German control of rations still continues, but their control of the camp is very lax. Places where you dared not trespass are easily accessible and I do not think the Germans round here intend to put up a fight.

Provided we can avoid any major action or skirmish I feel certain it will just be a question of the Germans walking out and our forces walking in.

May it be soon – The victory cake is baked and the sooner we eat it the better.

Tuesday 17th April – An Unfortunate Incident. During the past few days Muhlberg on Elbe and the vicinity of this camp has become a front line area, being some twenty miles ahead of our advancing forces on the West side of the Elbe.

As each day passes, aerial activity increases. Fighters and bombers fly continually overhead, unmolested by any activity on the part of the enemy.

It makes a very pleasant sight, seeing our fighter pilots continuously circling overhead from early dawn until late at night. Any attempt at movement on the road is immediately attacked without mercy. Any movement on the railway is immediately bombed.

But though our forces' activities thrills us, there are doubts and fears in the minds of all of us regarding our own personal safety. We wonder if pilots are aware that these blocks of buildings contain British and Dominion prisoners of war along with nationalities from every corner of the globe. At this stage in events, it is not to be wondered that we are keen on survival, and nothing must hinder our prospects of returning home.

Such an incident has occurred.

It is our practice, as often as possible, to send out fatigues to carry wood from surrounding forests. This wood is subsequently used for cooking purposes, as there is no coal. A returning wood fatigue, on Tuesday, comprised of British and Dominion personnel, were walking along the road by the side of the camp, when out of the sky came the tearing scream of a British fighter, which strafed the moving men carrying the wood upon their backs. There was one burst of machine gunfire and then he roared away, satisfied with his attack or realising that he had made a mistake. No further direct attacks have been made.

One South African, one British soldier, a British paratrooper, a New Zealander and a Russian Officer lost their lives. We also sustained eleven other casualties.

Rumours and doubt fill our minds but I am confident that the whole incident was a mistake, for a direct strafing of the camp could have been accomplished far more successfully up and down the main road, which is always crowded. There was only one burst, no more. Later we were assured that pilots did know all about the camp and where it lies. Nevertheless the letters POW have been inscribed on the rugby pitch and on various roofs of bungalows. Let us hope that nothing further happens, for our liberation is very close.

Thursday 19th April 1945. Today has been full of excitement. Shortly after our cup of German coffee and those two very thin slices of bread, which we affectionately term, breakfast, we went for a bath. This being exciting for this occurs once every two or three weeks and sometimes longer periods have elapsed. Coming out of the bath house I was in time to see squadrons and squadrons of British bombers advancing from every direction to a point North East of this camp. The name of the target we could not decide. A few minutes later shock after shock shattered the air, shaking our bungalows. Clouds of black smoke rose from the target area and the planes returned, their mission having been accomplished without so much as a spark of opposition.

Throughout the day there were the usual fighter patrols but we are accustomed to these and unless they open fire on some object along the roads or railway, we do not take a great deal of notice.

My afternoon passed doing a spot of cooking up at Jack's. Feeling confident that only a few days must elapse before relief, we decided to bake a small cake to have after our night meal of potato and meat pie. This was followed by a little German macaroni we had saved from the previous day, to which we added some milk, now very precious, and sugar. We decided to have the cake hot and our meal was a huge success, and I felt fairly satisfied, the first time for several weeks.

The evening provided us with real excitement. An ammunition train lying hidden in the wood close to the camp was well and truly strafed. A really remarkable sight, the planes diving within a few feet of the target and banking right over the camp. But the main excitement occurred after the planes had dispersed, for one by one the trucks exploded with shattering noise, shaking the bungalows and breaking several panes of glass and mirrors. There were twenty seven trucks all told and it took three hours before all was quiet again.

News at night was very satisfactory and Leipzig has fallen with the capturing of twenty thousand German prisoners, including the Chief of the German Police. All forces are advancing along a wide front on the Elbe. Thirty miles separate Russian and American forces at Dresden. Russian forces have also broken through the defences of Berlin. Things look very, very good.

Friday 20th April 1945. An atmosphere of expectancy still pervades the air. We decided to conserve what little parcel stock we still possess and if we are lucky we shall be able to have a good meal when liberating forces reach here. It is a "toss-up" who reaches the area first, Russian or Anglo-American forces. I hope that the Anglo-American forces make the grade, for we are not certain of the Russians. The morning passed quietly but during the afternoon loud explosions followed by clouds of smoke signified that something else was going on. It may have been the ammunition dump at Zeitung; it is difficult to say. The ground vibrated all through the day as if far off artillery fire was in operation.

During the evening, the camp Commandant Hauptman Honnig called a meeting of "Men of Confidence" of all nationalities to ask: "Whether owing to the speedy advances of Russian troops on Muhlberg we should prefer to move to the other side of the Elbe." All nationalities except the Poles elected to remain in the camp.

News at night was very good and the late bulletins, read by means of lighted paper, included a message from Eisenhower telling Polish and Russian prisoners of war to remain in their camps, and await allied forces, not to riot and not to loot.

Jim Barker, our assistant "Man of Confidence," came into our bungalow late at night with news that the Germans had elected to stay in the camp and not to evacuate. He also said that British troops had reached the outskirts of Dresden and Russians had reached a point not fifty kilometres from here. I rolled over cursing the hard boards and wondering how long it would take before my hips, thighs and torso sagged with flesh.

Saturday 21st April 1945. A definite anticlimax to the excitement of yesterday. Air activity was slight, and gazing out through the wire watching for something, which did not want to hurry itself. War seemed a long way away.

Sunday 22nd April 1945. There are many rumours. Victorious drives sweep on around us. There is a distinct rumble of guns far off, but definitely guns. The potato guard is standing by. The Germans are expected to move tonight.

Monday 23rd April 1945. Last night Russian forces arrived in this camp. Artillery and machine gun fire woke us in the early hours of the morning. A Regiment of Cossacks galloped into camp at 6.30 a.m. today. Had a celebration breakfast consisting of potatoes and a small cake. Russians broke through the wire attacking potato clamps. We were called out and after an hour's struggle, managed to prevent further influx of potatoes. There was terrible chaos outside, and Russian PoWs left to make their own way back. Murder, looting and revenge were practised around the countryside, though I think there were considerable amounts of suicides.

Every conceivable type of food was brought into camp, robbed and looted from the surrounding countryside. I was disgusted and waited anxiously for some law and order. But there seems to be no control by our leaders.

On 23rd April, when the Russians liberated the camp, an American Jeep managed to get into the camp. It was soon escorted back to the American positions. But before he went, he asked us to throw him papers with our names and addresses on. We did this and I was astonished to learn later, that my mother knew at this point that I was still OK. The American GI must have been very busy letting our kin know.

Tuesday 24th April 1945. An overdose of potatoes made me violently bilious last night and all today. Men are forbidden to leave camp but there are plenty of escape holes in the wire. There is no difference in rations; skilly [peas] potatoes, and more potatoes at night. No wonder a man fancies a chicken. But food has no interest for me today.

Wednesday 25th April 1945. At 11 a.m. I was out through the wire, pack on back looking for sugar and chickens. It is obvious that unless you look after yourself, potatoes and peas will represent your meals.

My final entry is 25th April 1945. After that there was no time to write anything else. I was too concerned with survival, as our position was a little precarious. We were still on the wrong side of the wire, although we could get out, there was always the risk of capture, this time by the Russians. We were also on the wrong side of the dividing line between British and

American forces, and the Russian. It was soon obvious that these lines would be firmly held and separate.

At last we were marched out of the camp carrying and trundling our limited possessions."

Dick had been in Stalag IVB for a year and a half. It was one of the biggest POW camps in Germany, located 5 miles north east of Muhlberg on Elbe, next to the village of Neuburxdorf. Dresden is to the south east and Berlin to the north, in what became part of East Germany after the war. Tony Vercoe described it as, "a crowded pestiferous monster of a place." [p.1] It has been reckoned that POWs from 33 different countries were imprisoned there at one time or another. In April 1945 it had 30,000 detainees. It is thought that about 3,000 Allied prisoners died there. When the Russians eventually took it over they used the facility to imprison captured Germans.

I am grateful to the Rijksmuseum, Amsterdam, for allowing me to use this image showing the entrance to Prisoner of War camp Stalag IVB.

A "Man of Confidence" was an officially recognised position in POW camps. He was the leader of those imprisoned, normally a higher ranking officer, who would be the official go-between for transferring information from the German Commandant to the prisoners and vice-versa.

At the site today no buildings remain but there are information boards which help visitors locate significant parts of the camp, which is now largely forest covered. The nearest village, Neuburxdorf, has a POW cemetery and a memorial to those who lost their lives.

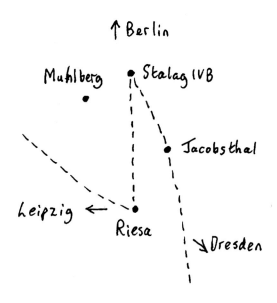

In Muhlberg itself, there is a museum with detailed display boards written in German, with photos, plans and information as well as some artefacts. A research group uses the museum as a base and some of their information is available in English. As Stalag IVB was such a big camp with so many prisoners held there, in more recent times its history has become well documented on a range of internet sites.

The interest that Dick had taken in theatre performances whilst in Italy was maintained in Stalag IVB, along with his friend Leo. On Christmas Eve 1944 the Company and Guests of Barracks 53B staged an International Cabaret, with an elaborately designed hand written programme. [Dick himself was in Barracks 23B]. Dick took female parts again, in a whole series of other music hall style productions.

While he was in the camp, Dick recorded the contents of various parcels he received, both Red Cross and personal, which included a number of deliveries of cigarettes from his mother, some redirected from Italy, as well as books, notebooks and pencils.

Also in Stalag IVB at the same time was Ray Newell, an artist who drew scenes of camp life for the wall magazine "New Times," as well as personal portraits in exchange for other goods. Ray would draw in what ever medium he could lay his hands on and on any kind of paper that was available, which was commonly the brown wrapping variety from incoming Red Cross parcels. The successful American post-war writer, Kurt Vonnegut, was also a prisoner in Stalag IVB.

The Reverend A.W. Ishee, another American, who was imprisoned at Stalag IVB early in 1945, commented in his memoirs on what he saw as the preferential treatment that the British POWs enjoyed. "The Germans treated them quite well. I found out later that the reason for the Englishmen being treated so fine in that camp was due to the fact that the Germans worked through the English to control all of the rest of the prisoners." [p.47]

If preferential treatment was really what the British were receiving, then the Germans certainly knew where they wanted the line to be drawn. Shot dead for straying out of bounds for a few strawberries does not sound very tolerant. Chris reminded me that her father told us later on that he also remembered someone being shot dead for trying to retrieve a football that had ended up in an out of bounds area of the camp.

The Reverend Ishee also had an interesting take on the events of the morning when the camp was finally liberated by the Russian Cossacks. "Buddy, I have never seen such a colourful bunch of troops riding horses as those coming towards our camp......They were all laughing.....I will never forget how that Russian in the front reared up his horse, pulled out a pistol, and shot the lock on that gate. He shot it again. Then he reached out and kicked the gate. With the help of the horses the Russians forced the gate open. [p.68]

> *"I seemed to lose contact with all my close friends, except Paddy. I don't think I ever knew his surname. We had acquired a wheel barrow onto which we put our possessions. After marching all day we came to a town between Leipzig and Dresden called Riesa. It was fairly badly mauled. It became known that we were to be put into some German barracks. Paddy and I were not in agreement with this and at a convenient moment slipped down a side street and hid.*
>
> *Wandering around later, we found a tobacconist's shop. Cigarettes were always a problem so this looked a promising place. We knocked and when the frightened Germans answered, we explained we were British prisoners looking for a billet. This seemed to them a better bet than the revenge crazy Russians. We were admitted voluntarily, arranging for us to sleep in the shop. The arrangement worked well. We would answer the door to Russian marauders, explain we were British POWs and they would shake our hands, back slapping all round and go away. In return the Germans would supply us with cigarettes. They slept in the basement of this three storied building.*
>
> *We had to survive as best we could, scrounging and stealing food and supplies. It was dangerous and at times life risking. Russians shot first and cleared the bodies away later. They did not differentiate between stealing Germans or British. We had no idea how to get home and were living in a chaotic world.*

V.E. [Victory in Europe] Day came, not that we knew until a Russian tank commander, looking for billets for his men, called at the shop and told us. The frightened Germans showed him upstairs and to our astonishment, in a town where hardly a house had not been looted at some time or another, the rooms were perfect. They were the living rooms of this family. Even the tank commander could not believe it. Dirty and travel stained, as were his men, he decided to sleep in the shop with us and left the rooms untouched.

Our presence had saved their home from being vandalised and looted. The cigarettes given were a cheap price.

The tank commander instructed his men to bring food and they brought what looked like half a cow, asking the Haus Frau to cook it. After her initial horror, he tempered his request to cook enough for a meal to celebrate V.E. Day. I had been looting in the larger residential houses and had acquired silver plated cutlery and serving trays, so the banquet was served on these, plus plenty of vodka etc. Paddy and I kept sober. Russians are very unpredictable when drunk. After, we all fell to sleep. We were woken by the sounds of tanks on the move, taking pot shots at random. Our Russian friends had left. Fortunately they left a lot of food behind, which came in useful. By this time we had become friendly with the Germans and would sit with them in the basement rooms and they would distil Schnapps, which would drowsily send us to bed.

Guards at the barracks, where many were being held, did not bother much with outsiders and we could talk to our friends behind the wire. I found Tom Summerfield and Leo Mundy in a park or wood [it's a bit hazy now and hard to remember]. I was able to give them some cigarettes but did not see them again because things started to happen.

Within a couple of days, I was walking along a road, when I met an army padre who informed me there were trucks at the end of the road to take us to allied lines. I dashed back to the billet and told Paddy. Paddy, a regular army soldier, single with no ties, thought for a moment, smiled and said, "You go Dick, I'll take my chance here." He had become fond of the Haus Frau's daughter. I often wonder what became of him but I shall never forget his friendship.

Collecting my kit and amongst real tears of regret and wishes of luck from this German family I sped to where the trucks were. I was lucky and managed to clamber over the tailboard of the last one before we moved off. I understand we were swapped for Russian prisoners on a basis of ten Russians to one British. Things were rapid after that and memory a bit clouded, as I was in a sort of daze. Two things stand out. The sheer whiteness of the American bread and the sheer exaltation of seeing the white cliffs of Dover, from the observation nose of a bomber. If the feeling of "being on a high" is like that, then I was on a high!

Soon I was rekitted; railway pass to Liverpool, ferry across the Mersey, No 14 bus to Liscard, walk up the familiar Monk Road to No 20, and an emotional reunion with my mother and my favourite, scrambled eggs on toast for tea."

Dick recalled and wrote this last section in 1995, as well.

Riesa was a small town about 15 miles south of Stalag IVB. It would have been a hard day's walk, especially when not in the peak of condition and pushing a wheelbarrow. I find this last section extraordinary. After all they had been through, their future still hung in the balance and the decision to leave the group and go it alone could have been so critical, yet must have been taken on a whim, or at least as a result of an instinctive gut feeling for self-preservation.

This lead to some improvisation on his part and he even owned up to a bit of looting in some of the empty houses, which had no doubt been vacated by their owners when they realised that they would be over-run by the Russians, rather than by the British. There was a great deal of movement of refugees in mainland Europe at the war's end.

Chris says that her dad told her about an episode which did not make it to his final script, in which he found a cow and decided to milk it. Having secured something to sit on and a vessel of some sort to catch the milk in, he literally tried his hand at milking a cow for the first time in his life. Under blackening skies, a sudden peel of thunder startled the cow, sending the stool, container and the milk flying.

As it turned out, Dick might arguably have saved himself the additional trauma of the billet and still found himself leaving town with Tom and Leo, had he stuck with the rest of the group. What strikes me is that it is during this time they were even more vulnerable to circumstance. When the rule of law breaks down and there is anarchy and chaos, you really don't quite know who to trust. At least within the camps there was an ordered way of doing things and as subordinates, you knew who you were responsible to and indeed, exactly who had jurisdiction over you and what your rights [however limited] and your duties were.

On the other hand, had he not decided to leave the group, we would have been denied the poignant story of the billet. Mutual interest led to conviviality and eventually to friendship between enemies and even a possible love affair. You could hardly invent a better fictional script. It is such a powerful finale.

When Dick and Paddy sat down to eat rather large pieces of cow with Germans and Russians at that bizarre feast in Riesa, the official final acts of the war were being played out elsewhere. The Germans surrendered in Italy on the 2nd May and in Europe as a whole on the 7th May. In Britain, rallies, street parties and a public holiday marked the official V.E. Day celebrations the following day. The war against Japan was brought to an abrupt end on the 15th August, after the Americans had dropped atomic bombs on Nagasaki and Hiroshima.

What an amazing contribution to the survival of so many servicemen the International Red Cross made. In conjunction with the Order of St John as part of The Joint War Organisation, the British Red Cross, mobilising many volunteers in the process, ended up distributing 20 million food parcels to imprisoned troops during World War Two.

The treatment of POWs was governed by the Geneva Convention, agreed in 1929, though Russia had not signed that treaty at its birth in Switzerland. Germany used this as a pretext to treat Russian prisoners a lot more harshly than Allied Western POWs, along with the claim that they were from an inferior Slavic racial group. The level of neglect and brutality of the treatment the Russians received is indicated by the figure of 3.3 million deaths out of 5.7 million detained, compared to 8,348 deaths out of 232,000 Allies held.

Tony Vercoe describes the Russian POWs in Stalag IVB thus, "In the worst cases, these poor creatures, hollow-eyed, skeletal, already dangerously infected and emitting a powerful stench of decay, stood unmoving like gaunt scarecrows or drifted slowly by as upright shuffling corpses. [p.50] Quoted in the same book, Fred Heathfield adds, "For some time the Russians had been taking out their newly dead to prop them up on parade to draw their meagre rations." [p.176]

It will have struck you by now that what started out as my book about Dick Jones's life has gradually become his book about his own experiences. I thought initially I might rely on extracts from his accounts to provide some pithy reminders of what it was really like to be there. As things progressed, not only did it become obvious that I needed to include more of the original script than I had first intended, but that, actually, nobody was going to tell his story better than he was.

So, in the end, I've included almost all of his narrative and made no changes to it. I have put in some facts about places and events, some of which Dick would have not had access to at the time. I think that by the time he got round to telling his story, he no longer had either the energy or the inclination to do any extra research for himself.

I am aware that my own observations during the recounting have become fewer as it's progressed and I'm happy that this is how it should be. However, when he reached home in 1945, he did not revisit his notes again for about forty years, so for the moment anyway, it is left to me to pick up the story again.

I had an idea, when I started to piece together my thoughts for this book, that I might re-trace Dick's steps, taking photos all the way. I was quickly put off a trip to Libya, however, as that country is still in turmoil at the time of writing and the official advice is "just don't go there." As I am somewhat less intrepid than Dick was, that was all the advice I needed to stay at home, in the comfort of my own computer chair.

I then thought, should I hire a car and travel through Italy and Germany? I found that I can actually trace Dick's journey pretty adequately from here too, using the world-wide web and its attendant mapping services. This means that anyone else who is prepared to conduct a bit of detective work can do the same, of course, right down to finding photos of the places as they look today. I'm sorry if it sounds like a cop out, but in the end it just wouldn't have added anything meaningful to what is recorded here already.

5. Rehabilitation.

The social life Dick had left behind in Wallasey was quickly back into full swing, it seems. By Christmas 1945 all the friends were back home; Gerry Roughsedge, Mick Harris, Bob Fish, Eric Harvey and Dick were re-united.

Dick Jones, back from the war.

Eric remembered how Dick was at this time. "After the war Dick was muddled. It had definitely affected him. We went to the Queen's Arms every Friday night. He was never a drinker. He went to scouts every night. He spoke openly about his war experiences. He had not been a regimental bird at all. He went in as a gunner and became a bombardier. He promoted himself to get a better deal in POW camp and he was backed up by the others. He was not a stickler for rules."

Dick pictured at a school, or more likely, a scout event soon after the war.

War time for the friends had started out the same but ended up very differently. Dick had appeared to suffer most, by comparison, though no doubt they were all just delighted to have come back alive. I think it's fair to say that if it was possible to have a good war, then all his close friends had had one. It was certainly possible to have a bad war and survive it. Dick did just that.

Dick re-opened his friendship with Joan Chaddock, which rapidly turned into a close relationship. Coincidentally, given Dick's most recent address in Germany, Joan was a tobacconist's daughter. Her father, Arnold Chaddock, had moved his family from Liverpool to Wallasey in 1925. Accurately forecasting that his job in insurance might not last the duration of the depression, Arnold had set up his own retail tobacconist business at Hackin's Hey in the city.

Joan attended Wallasey High School, her fees being paid by her family. Leaving school in 1936, she joined Martin's Bank in Liverpool the next year and was assigned to the Foreign Branch. The Chaddocks had to sell their house and they rented one in Wharfedale Road instead. Joan and her sister Marguerite, cousins of Eric Harvey, had become friends with Dick and his crowd shortly before the war.

While Dick was in the army, Joan was evacuated to Upholland to stay with her Auntie Ida, but in about 1942 the family moved again, this time to 68, Penkett Road, Wallasey, where they shared a large house with Joan's Auntie Jessie and her daughter, Eileen.

Dick and Joan became engaged in 1946. Marguerite told Eric how patient Joan had been with Dick after the war. Joan's father also took a liking to Dick. They operated an allotment together, growing vegetables on a plot of land next to their garden in Penkett Road, an area which was subsequently built on. Dick also drove Arnold to work in Liverpool for a time. David commented that he thought their relationship benefited from the fact that Dick was a son without a father and Arnold was a father without a son.

The betrothed couple took a convalescent holiday to the Isle of Man in 1946. Dick's Auntie Dorothy was staying in the same hotel, either by accident or design, but she acted as a chaperone to Joan throughout their stay, much to Dick's annoyance. Dorothy Roden was Dick's paternal Welsh aunt. The Welsh connection, however tenuous, still put in appearances at critical times, it seems.

Dick, the care free, pre-war, "one for the ladies," quickly became devoted to just one of them after it had all finished. In the last few weeks of her life, Joan told her younger daughter, with all the vehemence she was still able to muster, "I was determined to get him! I wasn't going to let *her* get him." Chris did not follow this statement up with the obvious "Who?" question, sparing her mother any further trauma at a difficult time, so it hangs there intriguingly, now never to be resolved.

Marguerite let it be known that Dick had once asked her, quite blatantly, "Do you fancy me?" to which she had replied, "I've always loved you as a brother." "Well, why not?" Dick had retorted. A growing friendship for Teddy that Dick had pondered over whilst he had been a prisoner, presumably related to a male friend. It was unlikely to be Maisie, either, who had literally closed the gate on him before the war. "A very pretty lady," Eric had observed about her. Nor was it Dorothy from Stourbridge. "Dorothy was just someone I got to know. Everyone went to visit Dorothy," Dick had told David, thus emphatically putting an end to speculation in that direction, at least as far as anything serious was concerned.

Joan's cousin, Eileen, told me that she did not get to know Dick until after the war. "We got on well together. We all went to dances at the Tower Ballroom," she remembered. "I reckoned to be a strong woman and I once challenged him to a fight. He was laughing so much he couldn't do anything about it."

It seems for a time, at least, Dick was almost living two lives. Re-united with his mates, he was also in love and courting. He was having a good time socially, picking things up again after an interval of six years. "He was the life and soul of the party," added Eric. "He played his mouth organ. Any sort of entertainment and he was there." Indeed, even E.W. Capleton had commented in his book about Dick's prowess on the mouth organ. He had performed at pre-war regimental evening entertainments at Hoylake Parish Hall, like the one held there in October 1939.

Yet alongside this public persona was a troubled young man. Barely old enough to go to war in 1939, he was still only 25 when he returned home, having witnessed and endured all that had been thrown at him during that time. At the same age, I was married and we had just moved into our first flat together, coincidentally also in Penkett Road. I was making mistakes as a rather tentative teacher, sticking it out and trying to establish myself in a very mixed and newly comprehensive school. I can not imagine how I might have dealt with similar circumstances to those that Dick had faced. I still felt so young and in no particular hurry to grow up.

In comparison, what a massive readjustment Dick had to make when he returned home. His old job at R.O. Edwards had been retained for him, but he was apparently not well enough to just go back and carry on. By early 1947, he was going by train from Monday to Friday and sometimes for a few weeks at a time, to stay at Peover Hall near Knutsford for a programme of rehabilitation. It was not clear, to start with, at whose instigation Dick attended there, or why it occurred so long after his return.

Formerly US Army General Patton's base in Britain, Peover Hall, described as being a resettlement centre for POWs in the post-war period, was not returned to the ownership of the Brooks family until 1950.

From Knutsford, Dick telephoned his fiancée and wrote frequent, lengthy and affectionate letters to his, "Dearest Joan." They are not always dated, the few that were being from early 1947. Joan, as she always did thereafter, kept everything, hoarding not just messages from Dick, but cards and letters from everybody else as well. Dick was a born romantic. There is something very, "Brief Encounter," about his writing. Try this, for example, dated the 23rd January 1947.

"It seems such a long time since we said goodbye to each other at the station this morning. We waved to each other as if we were never to see each other again instead of only a few weeks. But it was hard darling and you looked so nice standing there waving. I just wanted to jump out of that silly train and take one of those forbidden kisses – you know the cold kind which I am not allowed to have." He rather formally signs his name as, "Your own Richard," and adds six crosses for kisses.

Now that sounds like seriously in love - and expressed in such romantic, gentle, if not ridiculously over the top Hollywood style sentimentality. How much he must have craved that loving closeness all the years he was denied it, living in the strained company of lots of other men and with no women present, for so long. It's hardly surprising he went a bit overboard, now he had the chance to do so.

The letters are very thin on the detail of the treatment he received. Dick admits only to "my worries" but does not go into specifics. He talks about going for walks by himself but there is no mention of any friendships emerging with other occupants. They went on visits to factories, practised leather making and other practical skills and had talks on money management, which Dick could not quite see the relevance of to his own situation, though he did express an enthusiasm for the wood working option.

Peover Hall checked with R.O. Edwards about whether he was up to the job back home and received positive replies from them. It appears the patients were given samplers of various training courses for trades like plumbing and tailoring, lasting nine months or more and paid for under a national scheme. Dick showed no particular inclination to follow any of these courses either.

In the harsh winter of 1947, Dick describes train journeys through snow covered Cheshire. In letters dated in January of that year, he describes the set up at Peover Hall as though he has only been there himself for a short time. One wonders why it took nearly one and a half years after the war for this treatment to start. After an initial sun lamp treatment session in the Physiotherapy Department, he appeared a bit mystified about it himself, "I must be a little run down or something although I feel all right physically, darling."

If he was not sure about the nature of his treatment or the need for it, he was still disconcerted enough to write, "Perhaps all our worries and troubles will be behind us and we will be able to settle down again. I hope so darling and I am so sorry that I am such a nuisance to you and I wish things would sort themselves out."

He goes on to look forward to an imminent weekend at home. "It will be lovely to have a long chat to each other and discuss things with you and see if we can straighten things out." Brief clues like this are all Dick lets slip, that things are not quite as he wants them to be. The hint is that it is a joint problem that requires attention, but I suppose that was a perception which might not have been shared by all concerned and especially by Joan.

After his time at Peover Hall, Dick went to Walton Hospital in Liverpool for Electro Convulsive Therapy, a commonly used technique, in the 1950s and 1960s particularly, to treat depression and a range of other psychological conditions, by inducing a seizure. Electric Shock Treatment, as it became known, affected him sufficiently for Joan to have mentioned it to me soon after I had first met her.

His hand writing certainly changed, perhaps coincidentally - I would have to admit that mine has deteriorated too, as time has progressed - from the small, neat and precise written records of his war time experiences, to a much more expansive, wandering and less legible style, only apparent post-Walton.

On the eve of his treatment in Walton Hospital in May 1947, and in a very clear hand, Dick wrote, "Soon we shall be together again and perhaps things will seem ever so much brighter." The temptation is to conclude that Dick was suffering from post-traumatic stress disorder, though it hadn't become an identified condition at that time.

Unless you were visibly shell shocked, as indeed many were in both world wars, the sheer difficulty of coming to terms with war time experiences would presumably have been less effectively catered for over sixty years ago than it is today. The suspicion is that ECT was a bit of a blunt instrument. There is continued debate to this day about its advantages and drawbacks.

Eric added, "Dick got over the war regardless of his rehabilitation and the shock treatment, rather than because of it. When he was down he played the piano and listened to classical music." That would coincide with the experience of those who knew him subsequently. It was how he gave himself time to come round when he became upset.

Some commentators have suggested that POWs actually felt a strong sense of shame, in addition to the more obvious results of the hardship and privation they had faced. Sometimes it was acting service men themselves, who had not been captured, that advanced this view. As Tony Vercoe, himself a POW at Stalag IVB, put it, "They had allowed themselves to fall into the hands of the enemy and were at his mercy, worse, being unable to continue with their duties as fighting men, they were letting down their comrades in the field and somehow, also their families at home."

As if they hadn't already had enough to deal with on their return home. This extra psychological burden must have been an added nightmare, for those who succumbed to it. By comparison, the official Russian view was that any of their soldiers who had allowed themselves to be taken prisoner were actually traitors. Vercoe makes reference to an extract from the book, "Soldier Boy," in which George K. Zak wrote as part of his epilogue that there were, "…eyewitness accounts of the Russian prisoners held at Riesa near the end of May 1945 being marched by Russian soldiers to a nearby quarry where they were all executed by machine gun fire." [p.181]

6. The Family Man.

Dick and Joan themselves wasted no further time and got married on 13th September 1947, at Emmanuel Church, Seaview Road, Wallasey. Straight away, they were invited by Joan's parents to live with them at 68, Penkett Road and they were welcomed there too by Auntie Jessie [Arnold Chaddock's sister, whose husband Frank Cartwright had died in 1938] and Jessie's daughter, Eileen. Dick marked the occasion by carting the coal from Monk Road round to Penkett Road in a wheel barrow, no distance at all for a seasoned wheel barrow operator with relatively recent experience, though how many trips he made has gone unrecorded.

Their honeymoon night was enjoyed at the Exchange Hotel, Liverpool, which was a large and imposing LMS railway hotel in front of Exchange station. Dick would carry the hotel card, with their room number on it, in his wallet for the rest of his life. The holiday was continued at Babbacombe in South Devon.

A honeymoon snap from the family photo album. Dick's own caption read, "One of us pulled a face and the other just looked natural – on a day trip to Newquay – we paddled like a couple of kids."

Mr and Mrs Jones pictured on another visit to the Isle of Man, this time in 1948.

Their first son, Malcolm, was born in May 1949, followed by the twins, David and Jennifer, in July 1950 and finally by Christine, in May 1953. Chris's arrival had not been planned, though I'm glad she made it. It would certainly have increased the pressure at home in lots of ways, not least, financially.

Jennifer, David, Malcolm and Christine.

In 1954 the family moved to 76, School Lane in Wallasey Village and at the same time Joan's parents moved into a flat, a bit further down Penkett Road. Her father died the next year and her mother then re-joined the family at School Lane, where an extension was built after which Chris could have her bed back! Florence stayed with her daughter for the rest of her life, as a supportive, much loved and well integrated member of the family, in spite of the fact that she was bed-ridden for much of that time.

In 1956, Dick wrote his wife a letter. He was not away from home for any length of time and the letter itself is not located or dated. Perhaps he passed it to her. Perhaps he could only write what he really wanted to say. In a rather long winded and convoluted way, he told her that he thought she had put on too much weight.

It feels a little intrusive of me to read it, never mind to write about it, but Joan kept it safe along with all the others, knowing that they would be passed down. Perhaps it is a salutary lesson to all of us, acting as a little reminder to remove anything that we have committed to print but which we can't envisage ever wanting to share with the rest of the world at any time or under any circumstances and doing it while we are still in control of all our faculties.

Whichever way you look at it, it must have been a sad moment for Joan. She had given birth to four children in four years, raised them, moved house, looked after her ailing mother, kept home for seven people, prepared food for every meal, been denied an opportunity for years to get out to work or further her own career and provided marvellous support to Dick for years, through his troughs of depression and his rehabilitation.

When I first met her she had filled out considerably, compared to photos, like the ones above, that I had seen of her when she was much younger, but I guess that's hardly surprising. Chris said she "nibbled" while she made the tea and she would sometimes have to make tea for two sittings. By this time, although still a strong man with a broad frame, Dick had also acquired a bit of middle age bulk himself.

They were so funny over food. They would play a game with each other at every meal, including afternoon tea – surely the first thing to go if you want to partake of some disciplined slimming - but they were both in the same boat. It went something like this, "Have you had a cake, Joan?" "Why have you had a cake?" "Are you going to have a cake?" "I'll have one if you are having one," and so it went on until they had both had a cup cake *and* a fairy cake, washed down with at least two cups of tea. "More tea, Joan?" "Have you topped it up?" Yes, I've just done it." "Oh, well I'll have one, then.".......

I was a skinny boy and I stayed thin as a young man. I ate everything I wanted to and never put weight on. I exercised daily and could never sit still for a minute. Dick eyed me enviously. Having learnt to waste nothing in POW camp, he would proceed to strip every last tendon, piece of gristle, fat and skin from his piece of chicken, consume them all and then eat the parson's nose.

Self-consciously going through their little routine over the temptation of another helping and the same for puddings, I waded through two of everything without a second thought. Dick snapped at me, "You wait until you're 30," meaning that I would be showing signs of expansion by then. I just smiled. I doubt it, I thought, rather smugly.

This was a generation, of course, that had got used to a degree of food deprivation. Quite apart from the extreme hardships encountered in the POW camps, all sorts of foodstuffs were rationed during the war for those left behind, as the German U-boats tried to starve Britain into submission by sinking as much of her merchant shipping as possible.

The times of austerity and rationing continued into the post-war period as well. The situation became more relaxed as the 1950's unfolded and variety and quantity increased alongside a gradual growth in prosperity. Indulgence must have seemed a great temptation. The attitude of our parents' generation to food was generally characterised by maxims like, "don't leave any waste," "finish your greens," "don't be fussy" and "always leave a clean plate."

It is almost as though the age of plenty that we grew up in was, for them, too good to be true. There was, for those who had lived through those lean times, a perceptible feeling of guilt and embarrassment about openly enjoying plentiful food, not wishing to be seen to over-indulge and yet at the same time being increasingly tempted by the widening range of choice and the ready availability of it all.

No wonder that the attitude of post-war governments to food production and the agriculture industry was designed to ensure the country would never be so dependent on foreign food imports to such an extent again. It had already become an ingrained part of the national mindset.

Finally on that subject and at a much later date, while watching television one evening someone had commented on the lithe shapeliness of some actress or other, "on the box" and turning towards me Dick said, "You'll like to have a bit more of something to get hold of when you are older." So you see, I think he came round to Joan's way of thinking in the end. Perhaps she preferred him with love handles, too.

Back at School Lane, whether or not they already had a lot on their plate never prevented them helping out the extended family when it was required. In 1965, Marguerite's husband Geoffrey Tonkin, who worked for BAC Bristol on the development of the Concorde, amongst other projects, was seriously injured in a road accident in Portugal. Dick and Joan offered their niece, Joanna, a temporary home for some months in School Lane, whilst Marguerite helped Geoffrey to make what turned out to be only a partial recovery.

Dick's mother, meanwhile, had left Wallasey and now lived in Ormskirk, on the other side of Liverpool, but this did not prevent him from going to visit her religiously every Thursday evening, before he came home from work and right up to her death in 1969. David remembered his grandmother thus, "Rachel had long got rid of all her husband's possessions. She never got used to living in Wallasey. On later visits from Lancashire, Rachel never engaged anyone in conversation. She showed affection only to the cat. I believe she had been traumatised by events earlier in her life."

It has struck me as a little strange that not one single photograph of Dick taken before his scouting days has appeared to survive on his side of the family. As has been noted, Joan threw absolutely nothing away and indeed made a point of hanging on to every bit of family documentation that she handled. There does not seem to be even one picture of Dick as a baby, infant or young man passed on to him by his mother. How strange is that?

Eventually, Joan no longer had an elderly parent to consider either. With the tobacconists business sold, her mother, who had died in 1967, no longer around for her to look after, the demands of a large family still to be met financially and perhaps also ready for a bit of "me" time, Joan went back to work part-time, at her former employers, Martin's Bank, located in the city.

Remembering his childhood, Dick's "favourite elder son," Malcolm, recalled how, way back in the early 1950's, his father had a knack of making the relatively mundane into something special and dressing up an event into a real occasion, with a mixture of consideration and ingenuity. It was the "transformation of a salvaged rusty old tricycle into my 4th birthday present with the assistance of a tin of Valspar enamel paint [which was still on the shelf of the small workshop at Dudley Road] and leading me downstairs blindfolded in Penkett Road to its presentation in the front room sunlight." Another time, "…he presented me with a tape recorder and recorded message describing the circumstances of its acquisition." He was also "the organiser of concerts of stereophonic sound and nativity plays in the front room at School Lane. We became his stage crew, actors and advertising agents."

Dick's use of the term of endearment, "favourite younger/elder son/daughter," was just one of the light-hearted ways in which he would try to make each of his children feel individually special, for example when used on greetings cards at birthdays etc.

At the time I got to know them, Dick and Joan did not just have four teenagers. They seemed to have a whole neighbourhood of them. The boys had moved on from the "let's build a den" phase, which hadn't actually gone too well. They had used their hideaway to try to make bombs from chemicals and this was the only time the police had become involved.

Dick was livid, not so much, I think, about the nature of the transgression, but the fact that the police had been called on to intervene. He administered corporal punishment for the first and only time. Chris said she was petrified and yet she had had nothing to do with it. Malcolm reinforced the view that he was reluctant to use violence, but insisted "on equality, justice and fair play."

Dick was actually a very liberal parent. David thinks that he was keen to avoid the harsh regime he had himself grown up in. The children were always given latitude to express themselves, follow their own interests, both at home and school, make friends of their own choosing and indeed bring most of them home with some frequency.

As a result, there was a real bustle about School Lane. Each of the children had their own friendship groups and it appeared that they were all always welcome. I remember clearly scenarios where we would be hands in pockets on a street corner when it started to rain. Which house shall we go to? There would follow a litany of excuses. "My mum is poorly," "my mum says only two friends at a time," "my mum has got visitors staying," or "my mum is doing the hoovering."

It seemed that these were never considerations that were sufficient to limit social time at School Lane. It was open house and not just welcomed in, but tea and toast with jam for eight, thank you, provided on the plain green, 1940's style, Wood's Ware "Beryl" tea set. We did not think a lot about it but it was extraordinary generosity, regularly performed. They were not well off and they had plenty of mouths to feed already.

We were never once made to feel we were in the way. In the extended annexe behind the kitchen, where Dick had initially provided extra space for his mother-in-law, we could play our records or the transistor radio or get down to some serious snogging, coming up for breath only for the occasional interruptions, like when the coal scuttle needed refilling from the coal shed out at the back.

When a distraught boy in winkle pickers called Sidney came down to tell his friends Malcolm and David about the precipitous collapse of his relationship, interrupting the evening meal for seven in the process, he was ushered in and allowed to use the phone, which was in the hallway alongside the dining table. We all sat round trying to eat our meal not too self-consciously, while a tearful and desperate Sidney begged Ann to take him back again, from the other end of the telephone line. Dick and Joan supported him in his hour of need. They would do that for anyone.

Dick liked fish. He dug a pond at the front of the house and stocked it with goldfish and he bought a tank of tropical fish for inside, providing a plinth for it to sit on. One of the regular young visitors to the house must have put too much pressure on the supports and the whole thing crashed to the floor. It must have been a massive disappointment to Dick, to say the least. All was lost, of course, but once the dust had settled, or rather, the floor dried out, it was service as usual and no change to the open door policy.

The boys started their own band, practising in the garage when they could and Dick also acted as their road manager for a time. He had become a proud family man, but all was not well at work and sometimes it showed.

7. The Hotelier.

R.O. Edwards kept Dick's job open for him, as they were obliged to do, but they also supported him through his convalescence, when he must have missed many months of work. Further, they encouraged him by allowing him to take any wood home that he thought he could make use of. This he did, cycling through Liverpool with lumps of timber tied to his bike, sometimes taking it on to furniture and cabinet makers and sometimes using it himself.

He presented Eric with a nest of tables as a wedding present that still adorns his apartment today. For School Lane, he constructed a stereophonic "hi-fi" cabinet, fitted into the full width of the lounge below the window and housing his classical record collection, including the "Songs from the Shows" that he liked so much.

South Pacific and Carousel were particular favourites I seem to remember, however hard I have tried to erase them from my brain in the interim. The set-up housed his pride and joy, a Garrard deck connected to an improvised amplifier from a specialist supplier, which he was repeatedly rewiring to avoid hiss. We made full use of this system ourselves, of course, when the master of the house was not at home. We probably wore out more needles than he did in the end - or should I say Bang and Olufsen diamond styluses?

Then Dick's boss, R.O. Edwards, died and the business was sold to Goldbergs of London. The new owners made changes to meet the rising demands for chipboard and plywood emanating from the growing DIY market. Dick's expertise was in hardwood timber. He had been devastated by Edwards's death.

The impression I have is of an old fashioned paternalistic employer, who took real interest in his staff's well being. This had now been lost and Dick resigned his junior partnership in the company. To cap it all, Dick did not get on with one of the senior salesman at the company, whom he thought of as pompous and who, unfortunately, happened to live only a few streets away in Wallasey.

Already unhappy at the extension of his sales area that accompanied the changes, Dick started to think about leaving the firm. He could see that it was struggling and he did not hold out much hope for its survival. He and Joan hatched a plot to buy a large old house in New Brighton and turn it into a hotel. For the time being, they kept it a secret from the rest of the family.

Dick resigned just before the company went to the wall. R.O. Edwards ceased trading on 3rd April 1971. Including a few necessary interruptions, Dick had worked there for over thirty years. Belatedly, he realised that had he held out a little longer he might have received a compensation or severance package, which would have proved to be so useful in his new venture.

Dick sought legal advice and made a retrospective claim for remuneration. To cut a long story short, the eventual success of his application hinged on his preparedness to at least exaggerate certain aspects of his claim and at worst to lie. Dick was never going to do this. He was a proud and honest man. The findings of the tribunal expressed a critical part of the hearing like this, "The applicant himself, with the blazing honesty which has militated against his own case to an overwhelming degree, admitted that the statement in the reply was not accurate." Knowing him as I did, I would have expected nothing less from him.

David put it this way, "The company was in trouble and Dad thought he should make moves himself. He left and was persuaded to make a claim for redundancy on the grounds that he had been pressurised out. His claim failed because he was not prepared to compromise himself by telling a lie. He had too much integrity."

Dick and Joan sold 76, School Lane and bought a large red brick Edwardian house at the top of Dudley Road in New Brighton, securing a loan from the bank to give them time to make the necessary alterations before it could possibly be opened up as a hotel. Double fronted and with its original leaded lights and some fire places intact, it was a fine and commanding example of its type. It was just on the edge of the resort and about seven minutes walk from the station and ten from the promenade.

The "Sandpiper" opened for business in 1972, a certain Richard Wild from the Isle of Man stayed the night on the 3rd September and made the first entry in the visitors' book. It was always intended that their customer base would be businessmen - salesmen and company representatives, like Dick himself had been. They also perhaps surprised themselves by attracting the tail end of the regular holiday resort trade.

The business card advertising the Sandpiper Hotel.

Always an interesting location at the mouth of the Mersey, New Brighton as a holiday resort appeared to be on its last legs by the end of the 1960s. By then, its main fare had become a very seasonal day tripper market, as with so many other similar British resorts. Like almost all such UK seaside towns, it had struggled to retain its customer base in the age of the car, the aeroplane and package holidays abroad.

The building fabric generally was crumbling, the river and the sands were extensively polluted, attractions were closing down, the local authority was dithering, new investors could not be found and many Wallasey residents would have preferred to see that corner of the Wirral gradually become consumed by an expansion of the residential suburbs that already surrounded it.

Yet, amazingly, in those rather depressing times in the early 70's, families with young children still came on the train to New Brighton from industrial Northern England, the Midlands and Central Scotland, armed with buckets and spades and with the firm intention of hiring deckchairs, no matter what. If the weather was poor, as it often was, it could be such a dismal place to be. A handful of dogged and bedraggled holiday makers could be seen wandering between an increasing number of vacant units and derelict properties in search of a handful of greasy spoon cafes and some shabby amusements.

Not that Dick would entertain criticism of New Brighton. It was easy to get him going with an off the cuff remark about the "Last Resort," the title eventually coined by Martin Parr for his book of photographs of the area taken in the early 1980's. Dick would have none of it. He looked at New Brighton through rose tinted glasses at all times. He would take you on over even a slight and passing criticism of the town, or indeed of Liverpool, going through its own well documented problems throughout this time, as well.

Retrospectively, I really admire his steadfast defence of all he held dear, in the face of the incontrovertible facts, never mind the seemingly universal negative opinions and the increasing public ridicule, which was becoming the fashionable way to refer to Merseyside and its problems in the national media.

Dick practised what he preached, by using other local businesses in his own community wherever he could. Milk was delivered by the milkman long after most people were buying theirs at the supermarket. The newspaper was delivered from the local newsagent. Parts for failing electrical equipment were obtained from the specialist shop in New Brighton and basic foodstuffs were bought at the local grocery store.

This could have back-fired. Having been taken over by the son in the long-standing family business, the grocer's shop was always struggling, it seemed, in a doomed fight against the supermarkets. We noticed more and more items in the hotel kitchen cupboard that were, to put it kindly, perilously close to their sell-by date! For the biscuits and cakes, packed with sugar, that we and then our children were most likely to be sampling by then, this was not that much of a problem. We just hoped that Chris's parents were aware of any such discrepancies that might exist in the more perishable goods that they were still serving up to their customers.

Dick held out for the importance of belonging to a place very strongly, a condition I have come to share with him, as the years have passed. Perhaps he felt it particularly acutely because his personal links with home had been so severely threatened. Languishing in prison, unattainable riches like going dancing at the Tower Ballroom, a pint in his local and a stroll along the King's Parade promenade [arm in arm with who knows which girl?] must have frequently crossed his consciousness and affirmed his longing just to be back where he came from. Though we can all miss home during a prolonged absence, perhaps it takes an extraordinary set of circumstances to make it the desperately special place that it was for Dick.

If the holiday makers were disappointed with what they found on arrival in New Brighton, Dick would do his best to cheer them up. This was his forte. He was Master of Ceremonies in his own hotel. The former prison camp entertainer completely immersed himself in this new role. Dick and Joan arranged their duties so that Dick would prepare the breakfasts and Joan would make herself responsible for the optional evening meal. Ingenuity and war time cooking experience to the fore, Dick was in his element. What the hotel lacked in visible investment in modern conveniences, was more than amply compensated for by the sideshow he provided.

The back view of the fold-over business card advertising the Sandpiper Hotel.

Breakfast time was often pure theatre. Subjecting everyone to light classical or Rogers and Hammerstein in the background, Dick would talk everyone through breakfast so effectively with a mixture of tips about the local hot spots, "bigging up" the Granada

Bowl, Fort Perch Rock and Wilkie's Indoor Fairground and combining the sales pitch with a diet of gentle ribbing of whoever was present.

This ability to make fun of people in a way that they actually enjoy is an integral part of the make up of the extrovert showman and Dick had it off to a tee. It relied on an ability to think on your feet and a certain subtlety, born, I imagine, of sheer self-confidence. His guests were simply swept along with all the bonhomie. He mixed it up with the odd bit of sycophancy.

If he had a particularly opinionated and dogmatic guest who liked to stick his oar in first, Dick would breezily out-do him by contributing in the direction that had already been taken. He simply out-flanked them with more nonsense than they were spouting themselves. I don't believe he really agreed with half of what he was coming out with on such occasions. I think he did it to take the wind out of their sails and assume control of the situation again for himself.

He came out with the most extraordinary tripe sometimes [verbal, though he did like the taste of the stuff, too], but he kept his customers happy and no one seemed to care. It was a master class. Nobody was exempt when he was in full flow. His customers loved it and they loved him. Many of his visitors returned, time and time again, seduced by his charm and certainly not by the antique state of the electrics, the increasingly dubious "teas-maid" appliance on their bed side table, or the queue to use the only bathroom.

I loved taking my friends to the "Sandpiper." It often took a little time after the doorbell had been rung for someone to put in an appearance. This was partly due to the size of the place, but more likely because Dick would be answering the door and he would not, as we have already decided, be rushing towards the porch. As he rounded the corner in the hallway he could see his potential guests through the full-length glass of the interior double doors that cut down on the wind going into the hall, but sometimes seemed to be doing only a little for keeping the heat in for the rest of the house.

At this stage you could see him smile. He was planning his opening remarks and matching them to his new audience. They were welcoming in tone but they would be unmistakably and provocatively humorous in content. You were aware you would need to be on your guard and ideally have a potential riposte up your sleeve, but you also knew it was unlikely to be as witty as his initial burst. You felt instantaneously that he was genuinely pleased to see you and all your friends. They knew instantly that they were welcome there. They would all get a personal greeting and a firm handshake. Dick loved receiving visitors. He made you feel pleased to be there.

This is what some of my friends had to say about him, when I told them I was putting something together:-

"always a 'twinkle in his eye' and a humorous edgy comment within seconds when opening the door"
"He was certainly a lovely bloke and character who was ALWAYS interesting to meet and listen to, and welcoming."

The Jones's New Year's Eve Party was an important date on the calendar. Dick was in his element. He loved entertaining his friends. "Prankster, entertainer and show off," is how Malcolm described him, on such occasions. He would get in the crates of bottled pale ale and line up the glasses from the cabinet, giving each one a wipe with a dry tea towel along the way and Joan would prepare vol-au-vents, cocktail sausages, cheese squares with pineapple chunks on sticks and her speciality, the industrial-sized sherry trifle.

Their friends would arrive, the men in heavily creased slacks made of synthetic fabric, sports jackets and ties, the ladies with inflated hair do's in old lady colours, thick coats, an odd stole and rather excessive make up. [Chris does not know how I have the gall to make comment on other people's clothing or appearance, having made it my life's work to see through a complete existence in round-neck cotton tee-shirts and jeans.] Dick would adopt his best showman mode, quipping his way round everyone in turn. Porgy and Bess or light opera would permeate their way round the house, courtesy of the speaker extensions.

A handful of neighbours and other acquaintances would be invited to mix with their close friends, one or two of Joan's colleagues from the bank and a few relatives who lived within easy reach. Chris and I would always have something else to go to, but partly through obligation [I didn't really do obligation very much, to be honest], partly through politeness [which I like to think I did do] and partly because we liked some of their friends, who were always happy to ask us where we were up to with things, we usually stuck around for a bit. I did not really think very carefully about who these people really were. I rather wish now that I'd taken more notice of them at the time.

If only I could talk to them now. Would they have spilt the beans on their friend and given us the low down? Would they tell us more about the intriguing figures, who will remain enigmatic and peripheral, like Maisie and Dorothy? My guess is that in every generation, including our own, there are some instances, events and even misadventures, that will remain closely guarded knowledge within their own time, protected by the social group which is itself almost defined by having shared such experiences. We were not there to be part of it, so we will never know everything about it and that is just how it should be.

I've always thought there is something anti-climactic about New Year. Lucy Mangan, in the Guardian Weekend dated 4/1/14, described it as "the ending of one essentially arbitrarily labelled set of 365 days and the beginning of another one," though she did admit to feeling more energised by it than I usually do.

It has never really floated my boat, but we would go off about ten in search of our own friends, who would be somewhere around town. Dick loved it and so they would go for the complete package, including the countdown to midnight, the tall dark New Year visitor, the piece of coal, Auld Lang Syne, and the fizzy stuff in fluted champagne glasses that were only brought out for special occasions. Then they would clear up. I would like to think that we helped them when we got back, but my memory is a bit fuzzy about that.

The years rolled by. The boys had gone off to university, embarking on their own relationships and were living elsewhere. We all met up at the Sandpiper from time to time, with Jenny, who still lived relatively close by, seeing her parents most frequently. We saw a lot of them too, until Chris and I moved away as well, in 1982.

I was once asked by Joan to call them Mum and Dad. As an adopted son, I had already had two mums and dads and I couldn't quite get my head round having a third set. To call them Mr and Mrs Jones would have been far too stiff and I got the impression that because they had not invited me to do so, Joan and Dick was not going to be considered appropriate. I would have been happy with that but it never happened. At the time, I was too independent of spirit to be consumed so totally into my wife's family, so in order to retain my individuality, I never actually addressed either of them directly by name, ever again. My hang up, perhaps.

Nevertheless [and perhaps seemingly contradictorily] this was when I started to really get to know them both. Coming from a left of centre family myself, my politics did not always coincide with the views of Dick and Joan. This could lead, on occasions, to quite heated discussions. I don't know for sure, but I had Dick down as a natural Liberal and a floating voter [though I have noted that he had admitted going to dances at the Conservative Club in his memoirs] and Joan as a Conservative.

Notice, that that is not conservative with a small "c." Only recently, I discovered that Joan was actually a member of the Primrose League when she was younger, though I have no idea with what fervency she formerly advocated the Conservative cause. She was noticeably more anti-Labour Party in our "little chats" than Dick was.

However, I found them open minded, thoughtful and certainly not doctrinaire. There was an emphatic spontaneity about their perspectives, delivered by Dick with clear diction and no trace of a Scouse, or any other, accent [Welsh? Scottish?] and Joan with a slight Liverpudlian lilt. Dick only got angry during one of these rounds of shadow boxing on one occasion, probably prompted by something on the national TV news, when he told me not to be so "bloody stupid," in response to my interpretation of some event or other. I was secretly quite pleased to have got under his skin to this degree, but also a little taken aback that he had used a mild swear word. Though I swore a lot [not in his company, admittedly], I never heard him do so before that moment or thereafter.

The only other time that Chris and I managed to annoy him directly was when he threw a wobbler over a "Who" record. We liked to play our music fairly loudly on his excellent system [now a full Bang and Olufsen package] and we were half way through

Quadraphenia, when he burst in to object to Roger Daltrey's choice of words in the track entitled Doctor Jimmy. I have been advised at this point to let you to investigate the expletives for yourself, should you so desire, if, indeed, it is new to you!

He emerged into the back room from the kitchen, shouting, "I can't have that. Get it off. I'm trying to run a hotel here." The liberal credentials had taken a knock, but I had to admit he had a point. I thought it best not to take him up over it just at that moment. Perhaps we could discuss the appropriateness of lyrics and censorship at another time.

Anyway, it was a black mark for the speaker extension cables that had piped the offending section through to the kitchen and dining room. We had probably overlooked the fact that our music choice was now likely to be accompanying his filling of the dishwasher.

Generally, we got on very amicably over the tricky talking points of the day. Both Dick and Joan could always appreciate the validity of differing viewpoints and were respectful of those who thought differently from themselves. We had lots of good discussions in this way. They were both very good conversationalists.

Whenever war came up, as it frequently did, Dick avoided all personal references to it, except to say that they "didn't know what they were letting themselves in for." His view was tinged with sadness, above all other emotions. He repeatedly and resolutely thought that the protagonists should talk it out and not resort to violence.

Chris and I accompanied them to the pictures only once. It was a big mistake. We went to see One Flew over the Cuckoo's Nest, which was much heralded around the time of its release. What I did not know was that it contained scenes of electric shock treatment. Dick walked out. It was too much for him to bear. We felt so apologetic. As a foursome, we stuck to the television, thereafter.

We did not hear much from the mouth organ department as the years went on, but by this time Dick had added a rather cumbersome organ to his piano. The piano lived in his wood store, which in anyone else's house would have been the showpiece lounge, adjacent to the entrance hall. The organ, meanwhile, monopolised the space in their already cluttered hideaway at the back of the house, where we all watched telly together and where I escaped from time to time to catch up with the Liverpool Daily Post and the Wallasey News.

Dick was no longer drawn to music just to sooth any frustration or anger. He genuinely loved playing both instruments for their own sake and in such a languid and relaxed style that I was surprised that he ever got to the end of the piece.

Business at the Sandpiper ticked over, the garden blossomed on both sides of the central path and the adjoining gravel car park, the bedrooms were all painted, furnished and equipped and the kitchen diner performed adequately, given the limited space available for the arrangement. That set-up's greatest advantage was that Dick could regale his guests whilst he made them their breakfast and that was a master stroke – or maybe, it just happened that way! The showers remained half completed, but luckily the bath water was always stinking hot.

8. The Patriarch.

Dick and Joan's children and their partners provided them with eight grandchildren. Adam, David, Ian, Rachel, Ruth, Helen, Alice and Anna arrived and quite possibly in that order, during a relatively condensed and very fertile blitz of procreation in the late seventies and early eighties. Grandad found a new role and didn't he just wallow in it. Though I'm sure they all loved all four of their mums' and dads' mums and dads, they idolised Grandad. It was like having Father Christmas every day of the year, except, of course, they were not with him nearly that much.

Grandad, amusing his granddaughter, Alice.

All the four grown-up children had by now left Wallasey and so they saw their grandparents less frequently than no doubt everyone – and certainly the grandchildren - might have liked. No matter, he soon made up for it. Grandad took them to the fair, still chugging along in New Brighton. The indoor version was a protected Art Deco masterpiece in yellow and green to match the lido almost opposite, which was sadly no more. It had been augmented by a piecemeal attempt to replace the former outdoor fair, which had once occupied the surrounds of the New Brighton Tower Ballroom, until that site was redeveloped for housing. The recent add-on now occupied a chunk of pavement near the boating lake.

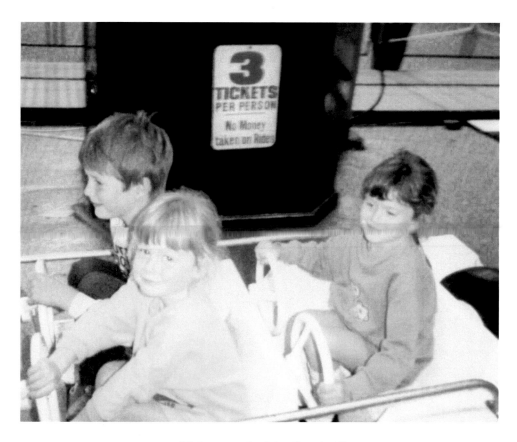

"Take us to the fair, Grandad."

At the time, the kids could not care less about the resort's cultural heritage. They just loved going to the fair with Grandad. He bought them candy floss and ice creams and he paid for their fairground rides. In short, he indulged them. He took them to shows at the Floral Pavilion Theatre and got so involved himself with the audience participation bits that he embarrassed the children. On reflection, the other grown-ups were not invited to any of these shenanigans. I'm not even sure that Grandma was allowed to join in. It was definitely Grandad's party.

He became the archetypal grandad, the self appointed patriarch of the family. To say that he loved the role does not do it justice. He absolutely revelled in it. In return, his grandchildren loved him to bits.

"Each year, my Grandparents would set out on their travels about England, visiting various offspring and siblings across the country. Year after year they would arrive in their Citroen Dolly, which smelt of hot leather seats. They would fill our living room with bedding and belongings, and fit very comfortably into our household. Their presence was the beginning of a week's holiday, a week of adventure shared with them.

My Grandma said, 'the secret to a successful relationship is to keep on going.'

One day, we went for a family picnic, on top of a hill in the country and all we had was a couple of blankets to sit on. I remember looking up at my Grandparents, who had positioned themselves rather cleverly back-to-back. When I questioned their positioning, my Grandad explained they were sitting like that to prop themselves up as they did in life. From that moment on I saw my Grandparents in this way.

Grandad must have been rich, he owned a hotel, he had a car and he always had a dispenser full of never-ending gold coins.

My Grandad loved to fill the hotel with chords and melodies from his organ."

From Ruth x

"Getting caught dancing on the glass table in the downstairs lounge early in the morning after stealing sweets.

They were the days that you never remember until somebody asks."

From Adam Jones

- *Grandad would sit in his arm chair in the lounge and we would sit on his knee and plait his long white side hair. We would pull his nose and he would shout out 'Not the nosy!!' in a funny voice*
- *Another thing I remember about him is that he always carried a coin box which was white and hexagonal in shape with different shapes for all coins. It was very exciting when he got that out.*
- *I remember him making us line up at the Christmas tree for our chocolates and I remember him letting us feed the fish*
- *I remember him going absolutely bananas at Ian for dipping bread in soup and I didn't understand what his problem was*
- *He made the best fried eggs*
- *He was one of the funniest people I have ever known*
- *He was one of the strongest men I have ever known*
- *He loved cake*
- *He loved ice cream*
- *He would take us to the pantomime and we would be so embarrassed as he would be joining in at the top of his voice*
  From Alice

Alice touched on the soup incident, or should I say, "**The Soup Incident.**" We were all sitting round for our evening meal, which was a regular occurrence, when we stayed with Dick and Joan. Ian dipped his bread in his soup and Dick told him off. Ian, being somewhat independent of spirit from the earliest time that it was possible to show such strong will, questioned the judgement.

Grandad went ballistic, not so much directed at Ian, but soon addressing us as his parents for failing in our duties to ensure he was not just well mannered but obedient. "You're too soft with him," he bellowed. Our philosophy, like Dick's, was non-violent parenting and dependence on reasoning at all times. If that did not work, we would withdraw our offspring from the situation until they had calmed down sufficiently to change their behaviour and were willing to apologise where necessary. It was pretty straightforward stuff, though I guess child rearing usually seems a lot easier with the benefit of hindsight than it actually was at the time.

Alice remembers it well because it was a "one-off." Dick's moods may have been intermittent; sometimes his own feelings were easily hurt by fairly innocent and apparently innocuous comments, but this was the only time he blew up at one of the grandchildren. Consequently, it acquired folklore status, in our branch of the family at least.

An emotional man, Dick, like so many who are on the front foot when undertaking a bit of verbal jousting, was sometimes a little susceptible to getting hurt himself. It was not general ribbing that got to him, as much as an unguarded or off the cuff remark that he then chose to interpret as a personal criticism. It could send him off in a bit of a sulk. After further discussion, Chris and I agree it was sometimes more than a bit of a sulk.

However, nobody is perfect and no-one could question his kindness. His generosity to his own grandchildren was sometimes extended to other people's as well. I have been reminded of a day out in mid-Wirral when it seemed, by accident or design I'm not sure, that hordes of our friends had descended on Brimstage Hall, with various offspring in tow and at the same time that Dick and Joan were there with Jenny. He bought ice creams for all the youngsters present. It was a simple act of giving, but one that was never forgotten by the recipients.

Grandad takes our part of the family on the Mersey Ferry.

If I'd thought a bit more about it, I might have had second thoughts about accepting his invitation to go on board a ship with Grandad. I should at least have checked the weather forecast and the state of the tides. His track record for boats was not that good; hit a submerged wreck soon after leaving port, encountered the worst storm for 70 years rounding the Cape, torpedoed by his own side and finally shipwrecked. It is reassuring to see that the ferry was equipped with a very visible lifeboat. Perhaps I gravitated towards it subconsciously when we were choosing our seats. Luckily, we got away with it this time.

9. The Hero.

The hotel operated as such for very nearly twenty years, after which time it simply became their home. The last entry in the visitors' book was made by a D. Stevenson of West Kirby, on the 16th February 1992. Dr, Mr, Mrs, Miss or Ms Stevenson had to do without a separate shower, because they never got finished, although one could take one while standing in the bath, if preferred. They remained as work in progress for two decades.

I had thought this was just a token gesture in the end, but David has corrected me since. Dick had discovered that there was insufficient water pressure from the feeder tank. Presumably, this made the whole business much more complicated and expensive to install. Even to my untrained eye, the plumbing implications, bits of which lay around throughout the period in half-wrapped and faded cellophane, looked horrendous.

They had also offered long term arrangements for a few elderly guests over the years. Presumably, these were people without a family of their own who had nowhere else to go and who maybe had put themselves at the mercy of the local authority or who could just about afford some very decent long term rates at the Sandpiper from their own savings. This was in keeping with the Jones's natural kind-heartedness. They must have known that they could end up nursing these vulnerable souls, or at the very least arranging their care for them when their health began to fail, but they did it anyway.

The rest of the family continued to visit Wallasey regularly throughout the 1980's and the 1990's and Dick and Joan also visited the outposts their family had landed in; West Kirby [later North Wales], Nottinghamshire, London and Berkshire. They arrived armed with thermos flasks, plastic pick-up cups with glass inserts, fold-up chairs, blankets, an add-on comfy car seat for Joan's bad back, tins of cakes [out of date Mr Kipling and Lyons chocolate cup cakes] and pocket money for the children from the now famous dispenser.

They arrived in the old blue mini and then when that died, a 2CV that they were given by a friend on a permanent loan. A hip and trendy car it may have been, but it looked a tad vulnerable to me, a sort of general lack of required robustness. When Dick nearly fell asleep at the wheel on the way to a family wedding in Bristol, Chris and I probably made the same decision independently not to travel in it again. On its way back across the Pennines at a later date, the roof rack fell off somewhere in the hills and their suitcase disappeared with it. Some kind individual eventually returned their belongings to them.

Dick stuck with the New Year's Eve party event until there were simply not enough people around to make it viable. That must have really hurt. He was so magnanimous and he genuinely wanted to give other people a good time. So determined was he to be generous to people in need that he invited lonely individuals who were otherwise destined to be on their own to join them for Christmas dinner. This pattern existed for a number of years, regardless of which members of his own family could also make it to the festivities.

I have no idea how he identified those in need, complete strangers to us, on the occasions that we turned up. Maybe it was through the church, St James's in New Brighton, which they had started to attend more regularly. I'm not sure this active religious re-awakening was sustained for very long. In fact I rarely recall any mention of religion in our discussions. I suspect that they were both rather tentative and lukewarm as far as any certainties of matters spiritual went.

Dick continued to see his old friends at the Victoria Hotel in New Brighton, which had taken over from the Cheshire Cheese in Wallasey Village as their regular Friday night haunt. Gradually, his friends started to lose their health and one by one they disappeared from the scene. I remember Dick taking a call about one of his close friends on the telephone in the back room at Dudley Road. I felt his sadness as he received the news that yet another one had lost his personal battle for survival.

Dick was soon the only one left, apart from the remarkable and admirable [and now ninety six years old] Eric Harvey, who still lives in Hampshire and who obviously could not get to the Cheese on a regular basis, though he has steadfastly made it to the scout's annual re-union and to Remembrance Day, year after year for decades.

Dick's proactive response was to go out and find some new friends. He joined the Manor Bowls Club, playing at Harrison Park in the summer months and indoors, at the YMCA, during wintery weather. He also kept up with his swimming as long as he could, perhaps finishing with that when it became too much for Joan rather than for himself. He was very considerate in this way, always wanting to make the experience a shared one.

Dick, with a new bowling friend, at the Manor Club.

Perhaps prompted by the existence of his grandchildren and questions they might shortly start to ask him, Dick set about sorting one or two things out. I guess there is a stage in most people's lives when they start to look back nostalgically and with reflection on their place in the overall scheme of things.

Though he attended the November Armistice Day march and service at West Kirby each year, he must have been the only one of the surviving old comrades from his regiment not to have any medals. In keeping with his previous determination to consign his experiences to history, he had not requested those he was entitled to at the appropriate time.

Around the time that he revisited his wartime notes and enlisted Joan's help to organise them, Dick wrote off to the Ministry of Defence for his gongs. After a series of letters to the Army Medal Office and the Army Records Office had been exchanged in a process that he began in 1985, Dick finally received due recognition nearly two years later.

In answer to a request from the authorities for more details, Dick replied that on his return home from the war he had "spent some time on leave and some time in several hospitals and was discharged as unfit. I had a small pension for some time and had to return to hospital in Knutsford and Walton." The fact that he was initially hospitalised by the army, then discharged and then readmitted to two further institutions was unknown to Chris and me, but it finally gave us a clearer picture of Dick's condition in the years immediately after 1945.

Dick put his medals in a small display case adjacent to the fireplace in the back room, where they kept company with a smart 149th regimental shield and plaque. He got them out to give them a good buff-up before each subsequent Remembrance Day. Dick was secretary of the 149th Old Comrades Association, effectively co-ordinating its continued existence with the chairman, John Cobb.

Now that Dick was showing a renewed interest in his wartime experiences, Chris and I arranged to meet Dick, Joan and his, "favourite elder daughter," Jenny, off the bus from Liverpool one day when it arrived in Leeds. All together, we made for the Leeds Armoury which is part of the National War Museum, where an exhibition of the wartime paintings of Ray Newell was being held. Thinking of others again, Dick had brought along another former comrade and friend's widow to share the day with us. It was a moving experience for everyone.

In 2000 it was decided to wind up the Old Comrades' Association. The numbers attending each year had inevitably steadily dwindled. Survivors were now all in their eighties and it was thought they should end the matter collectively and formally, rather than letting it just peter out.

Plans were made for the laying up of the standard at a ceremony on the 17th June 2001 at St Hildeburgh's Church in West Kirby. This would be followed later in the year by a final reunion for members on Saturday the 6th October and a last opportunity to officially remember old comrades at the memorial on Grange Hill in West Kirby, during the next month.

November 2000 was the time that David had decided to present Dick with the completed version of his war diary, which he had edited and had spiral bound. I drove Joan along the track up the hill on Remembrance Day, so that she could be present in her wheelchair when Dick laid the wreath at the memorial.

A word about this location is required. Grange Hill stands in the north-west corner of the Wirral Peninsula. It is a windswept location, as often as not. The views from the top are wonderful. The city skyline and its famous public buildings to the east, the mountains of Wales and the estuary of the River Dee, glistening in the sun light to the west and out beyond to the north, Hilbre Island and the Irish Sea stretching out to the horizon.

It is such an atmospheric spot. Add to the mix a good attendance of all ages arranged in a semicircle around a natural amphitheatre just below the peak, a reflective occasion to remember the fallen, flags fluttering in the breeze, solemn military music, Elgar and hymns. I defy anyone not to be moved under such circumstances, when, as your eyes drift out over the waves, "For those in peril on the sea," strikes up.

With his children present as well, Dick was feeling a little overwhelmed.

> *"With so many surprises it was difficult to control my emotions, especially in front of my Comrades. Five of us marched with the procession down the hill. The Scottish Piper who slow marched round the Cenotaph also led the Parade to the sound of his pipes. I gave the order "Eyes Right" as we passed the Rostrum, to be finally dismissed in Dee Lane."*

> *"As usual we gathered in the Concourse Library where several of our comrades, wives and friends were present including Lord Hunt who always makes an effort to attend. Again I called the party to attention and John laid the wreath on the Memorial.*

After the ceremony we all reconvened at the coffee bar and with Dick's other children present as well, David passed him the book in a plain brown envelope. It was a complete surprise to him and it left him visibly moved.

Dick prepares to lay the wreath on behalf of the Old Comrades' Association for the last time, in November 2000.

David presents his father with his completed war memoirs, with Malcolm in attendance.

Dick shows the document to his former comrades.

"My emotions were on a high which can only be compared with my feelings, when coming home from my incarceration, I saw the White Cliffs of Dover from the transparent nose cone of a Wellington bomber.

What can I say to express my deep thanks for all the efforts that have gone into making this day perfect? There seems to be no other way but to use a sentiment well known to each one of the regiment. This is the message sent by the Indian Regiments of the 4th Indian Division when the remainder of the Regiment - about 230 men – prepare to come home about July 11th 1945 from Greece, along with a gift of 52,000 cigarettes and 74 crates of beer:-

"SHABASH [Well Done]
149 GOOD LUCK AND BEST WISHES

So I say:- "SHABASH FAMILY AND FRIENDS"
[sorry about the cigarettes and beer]"

Though Dick's heroic efforts were now properly recorded for posterity, this was not the end of the story. The Old Comrades Association was formally wound down the following year, as planned.

The press were present again, when in June 2001 the remaining old soldiers said their official farewell to Hoylake. The Laying Up Ceremony was to be followed by lunch at the King's Gap Hotel in Hoylake, a few minutes walk from the parish hall and the Carr Lane regimental meeting place, where it had all started 62 years earlier. Dick's children and a good sprinkling of grandchildren were home again to mark the occasion.

The regiment would also continue to be remembered on a plaque designed by Sergeant Hubert Morris, first unveiled at Hoylake Town Hall in 1951 and moved to the new West Kirby concourse in November 1981. Since March 1991, another plaque had been placed in St Hildeburgh's Church.

A solemn occasion for Dick and his former comrades, in June 2001.

But not for long, as Dick entertains those attending for lunch at the King's Gap Hotel, including Joan, Steven Hesford, the local MP and David's wife, Judith Jones.

Dick did get to the 2001 Remembrance Day on Grange Hill, though this time Joan was not able to make it and Dick himself benefited from the provision of a chair which we had taken up for him in the car. The laying of wreaths would now be left to others to perform. His "favourite younger son," David, took his place on this occasion.

By now, Joan's health was beginning to fail her. She became very breathless after anything that could qualify as movement, eventually even from room to room in her own home. With high blood pressure and an enlarged heart compounded by back trouble and macular degeneration, she took increasingly to her bed.

Dick took charge, of course, taking her breakfast in bed daily and gradually assuming the role of her carer. At the time, we thought perhaps he was doing too much for her, encouraging her to see herself as an invalid, when possibly encouragement to retain some more self-sufficiency and mobility could have been better for her.

Dick did not see it that way. He remained the dutiful, loving and caring husband. As happens, under such circumstances, their world started to shrink. It became such an effort for Joan to leave the house, firstly with the help of a stick then with the wheelchair. The trips out became fewer and fewer, even when younger family members were there with their cars, to help.

Then, unfortunately, Dick himself became ill. A long time smoker, he was diagnosed with a cancerous tumour on the lung. Though he had given up cigarettes decades earlier, when the children were young, it seemed it had eventually caught up with him.

From being the prime carer, he was now increasingly in need of support himself. It was a shock to him, of course, but he was extremely low key, restrained, unemotional and matter of fact about it when he told us. It would have been the impact on his daughter he was considering at that moment. Already in his mid 80's by this time, he was informed they would not be intending to operate on him.

My father had been in a similar position a decade earlier and from diagnosis to his eventual death in 1996, he had enjoyed a further five years of life, most of it very good quality. He had remained stoical and positive throughout the experience and Dick was likely, I was sure, to do the same.

By the winter of 2007/8 Dick was himself bed-ridden. With local authority, NHS and family support, Dick and Joan - who was obviously not able to look after him herself, moved out of their former bedroom into hospital style beds in their former bolt hole – the small sitting room at the back of the house, where we had all sat round for years to put the world to rights.

Visitors came and went, to wish him well and effectively to say goodbye. Dick was determined to be in good humour, but with so little energy remaining to make it happen. I wrote a poem, one of a series over a couple of years, having been introduced to the medium by a colleague and for a short time finding it was a potent way to express my feelings. It coincided with a period when a number of our own "older generation" were coming towards the ends of their lives.

I am sharing it now for its relevance rather than its quality. I don't even know if it strictly qualifies as a poem, as scanning and the like were not what drove me. I guess it has a sort of structure to it, at the very least. What prompted me was when Dick told us about the little girl who had befriended him on his last visit to Grange Hill. She could spot a top-draw grandad, without a doubt. It was about Dick and I wanted to read it to him. By chance, Eric Harvey and Joan's sister, Marguerite and one or two other friends were also present so there was quite a gathering and I read it to the assembled company.

Hero

Slowly up the hill, at his pace, we walked,
him with his stick and his medals,
taken, very deliberately, from their modest display case
the night before, for their final polish.

Did he remember, as he rubbed the metal,
the man he argued with over a desert trench,
only to see him blown in half by mortar fire?
He did not mention it.

We approached the windswept cenotaph,
the sun gave way to squall. He sat down
on a fold up chair, legs covered by a rug,
protected from lashing rain by the shield of his family.

Had he remembered, as he rubbed the metal,
the dysentery in the ship's hold, as the prisoners
fought for air, packed tight in their own mess?
He did not mention it again.

The band struggled to hold their notes.
He sat and thought of friends he'd lost,
whilst younger folk dried their eyes on their sleeves,
straining over sodden hymn sheets, through misted glasses.

Had he recalled the moment the ship was hit?
The torpedo sent the hatches high above,
crashing down on those next to where he stood.
If he did, he kept it to himself.

As we walked down a little girl approached,
put her hand in his and looked up in his eyes.
"Are you a real war hero?" she asked, innocently.
He smiled and thought and said," Well yes, I suppose I am."

Did he revisit lost years in the camps,
the lice that teemed and crawled about his frame,
pinned to a table, the abscess slashed with a blade?
If he did, he chose to leave it there.

Finally, this old soldier's last address,
to comrades, just three left, around the wreath,
where, centre stage, he found the right words yet again.
This was the last time. He had to leave it there.

Dick thanked me and sank back onto his pillow. I felt there was some mutual respect there, at least; something that I had not always been confident had existed in the early years, as we gradually got to know each other. He died in Arrowe Park Hospital at the end of March 2008.

The day after his funeral on the 1st April, the family took the urn containing his ashes down onto the shore below Harrison Drive, exactly to the spot where I had been playing football with my friends on a warm spring day in 1967, when his "favourite younger daughter" walked past on her way back home from the Derby Bathing Pool, to start her paper round. This time, Chris sat in the car and held her mum's hand, watching while we took turns to scatter the ashes on the incoming tide as it crept up the channels of the sandbanks, known locally as Mockbeggar Wharf.

Malcolm read, "I must go down to the sea again," by John Masefield and there seemed no more appropriate way to say goodbye to the son of a ship's captain, who had come from a long line of seafarers. The sea had nearly claimed him much earlier in his life, but he had survived, at first struggling to put his demons behind him and then spending the rest of his life helping others and spreading happiness and goodwill around him wherever he went.

Chris told me afterwards that as she sat quietly in the car with her mother, she noticed that her wristwatch had stopped. After the event and when everyone else had gone back to the Sandpiper, Chris and Jenny returned to the spot at the edge of the now incoming tide, so that Chris could say her own goodbye. On her way back up to the promenade she noticed that her watch had started to work again.

On the beach at Harrison Drive in happier times, during the summer of 1979.

On these sands, Dick and Joan had sat in their fold-up chairs and entertained their grandchildren, dishing out the orange juice and the chocolate mini-Swiss rolls. They had laughed and Dick had teased and I never saw them happier than in that place and in that company. Joan would join him there for the final time a year and a half later, in November 2009. As Chris had said, when she recalled visiting North Wales to help support Jenny, as she cared for her mum in those difficult last few months, "Mum used to sleep with his photo at Jenny's house. She just wanted to be with him."

And now she was.

Only two generations were present on the foreshore this time. The grandchildren were there in force again, though. What fabulous role models Dick and Joan were for us all and especially for these young people. Their's is the true inheritance from this fine couple, not measured in money or heirlooms, but in memories and the mutual love and affection that they will hold onto for ever.

I tried to capture the moment for myself in December 2009.

Come Together

I first played here in '57, took sunburn home that day.
Soon after, rescued from a shrinking bank of sand,
bundled unceremoniously under a burly arm,
without a thought for this now special land.

Peered over the wall in '67 into the noisy throng,
at the swimming pool, for a glimpse of their daughter below.
The wind took our football for miles as she scurried past,
embarrassed, with a fixed, half smile. How could we know?

Lying here in summer heat in '87, squinting through bright sun,
to see these two, entrenched in fold up picnic chairs,
their grandchildren's laughs and squabbles on the sand,
with cushions, thermos, Mr Kipling and éclairs.

Proud leader, animated by his young tribe of eight,
attentive assistant with provisions and endeavour;
dependable, sturdy, unyielding as the distant lighthouse,
as gulls wheeled and warned "Nothing lasts for ever."

Twice more of late we have returned
to this location, their most favoured treasure.
In the end barely a year apart,
they'd rather have come together.

Again a solemn group, eighteen all told,
only two generations here this time.
"I must go down to the sea again",
shimmering through the tears of each line.

At the edge, the tide snakes up the channels
and mud takes over from firm sand.
Gusts from the north, surprisingly not icy;
despite our best intentions, lift ashes from the strand.

Close your eyes, hear the lapping of the waves,
recall the children's shrieks and mock admonishment
from these two, never happier again,
as the tide now claims all they have to send.

Joan and Dick Jones.

So, let's raise a glass to an old soldier, his wife and his friends and all those who spent six years at war so that we might live in peace. In the process, they gave up what they might, under normal circumstances, have expected to be some of the best days of their lives. How lucky we were that Dick survived his ordeal to fulfil the roles of husband, father and grandfather so supremely well.

And not quite finally, Dick, thank you for your recollections, so vividly expressed. I hope you don't mind me tinkering with them. I'm leaving the last word to your granddaughter, Rachel.

The jigsaw pieces of my family puzzle have been broken up now, and some of them are missing. Most noticeable is the loss of the piece bearing our family's heart: my grandad. He was many things, my grandad. Many different things to many people. To his comrades at war, he was a loyal, dependable, brave soldier – worthy of the honours and medals bestowed upon him. To his friends, someone to share a pint and a story with. To the guests at the hotel he ran for many post-war years, he was the host-with-the-most: the breakfast chef who served it up with a smile. To countless children in his Parish, once a year he became Father Christmas. Wearing the red suit, he would convince even the most doubtful 4 year old that Old Saint Nick would be on his way on Christmas Eve. To his children, he was a role model: someone to impress, whose footsteps should be followed, whose mould should never be broken. To his wife, he was everything. A diamond, a soulmate, a friend and a companion.

And to me?

Pocket money giver; Oliver Twist-watcher; nose-stealer; story-teller; hugger; smiler; loud-snorer: Grandad.

Since his death, I've tried to remember these things above all else. When images of his withered shell in the hospital bed steal their way into my mind, I push them away with memories of 'The Little Engine That Could' being read to me as I drifted calmly off to sleep. Safe. When the reality of him being gone hits me, I remember him chasing me and my cousins around to 'steal' our noses; holding his thumb between his two forefingers to trick us, while we giggled and screeched "Not the nosey, not the nosey!" Our favourite pastime.

And his car. The mini. We would all pile in on a Saturday – more of us than I'm sure is safe, or even possible. Trilby on, he would drive us off to the swimming baths, where we would play and splash until the buzzer told us our time was up. Then we would drive to the sea front. I never understood it at the time. We wouldn't get out of the car, but would sit inside and gaze over the sea to Wales – steaming up the windscreen with our drinking chocolate. Despite its weakness and its distinctive flasky taste, I remember this as the best drink. Not because it was especially nice, but because it was the taste of Saturdays with my grandparents.

Grandad's death left a gap in all our lives, but most significantly it took away grandma's sparkle. Without him by her side, her zest for life faded – replaced by a taste of grief and loss. She wanted to follow him – to have him by her side again. The photograph by the bedside wasn't enough.

I wish I could piece together the puzzle of my childhood in its original form, but I know I can't. There are pieces missing which are irreplaceable. But when I look back on the memories of my childhood picture, I'll always smile.

From Rachel Coleman

Acknowledgements

I would like to thank the following individuals and organisations who have kindly helped me during the preparation of this book:-

Dick Jones, because, as will have become all too apparent, I have wrapped my story round his own.

Joan Jones, Dick's wife, for making me feel so welcome in her home, when I was a young man and at a time that she was under a lot of pressure.

David Jones, Dick's son, who has provided me with access to family records and photographs, as well as the results of his own research into his family's history.

Malcolm, Jennifer and Christine Jones, Dick and Joan's other children, for sharing their impressions of both of their parents with me.

My daughter Alice, my nephew Adam and my nieces Ruth and Rachel for adding their written contributions about their grandad.

My friends, for taking the opportunity to have their say about my father-in-law.

Eileen Cartwright, Joan's cousin, for her memories of the post-war years.

George Chatziioannou, at Methoni TV, Greece, for giving me permission to use a photograph of the Sebastiano Venier.

John Cronin, the Editor of the Hoylake Junction on-line newsletter, for circulating information about the Hoylake Horse to his readership on my behalf.

Alec Dauncey, for quizzing his father [94 at the time of writing] about the activities of the 149th in Hoylake during the summer of 1939.

Cecile van der Harten, at the Rijksmuseum, Amsterdam, Netherlands, for sending me a high resolution picture of the entrance to Stalag IVB for me to use in this book.

Eric Harvey, Dick's lifelong friend, for welcoming us to his home and for telling us his own story.

John Hutchinson, a Wirral resident, for contacting me about the memorial on Grange Hill.

Eira Reid, Dick's sister, for her brief recollections, as recounted to Jenny, about Dick's childhood.

The Alexander Turnbull Library, of Wellington, New Zealand, for giving me permission to use a photograph of the Sebastiano Venier.

Bibliography

E.W. Capleton, SHABASH, The War Story of the 149th Reg' R.A. 1939-45, 1963, Tinling, ASIN B0014A14SW.

Warwick [Bert] Ibertson, In Search of Harry, [unpublished internet account].

Rev. A.W. Ishee, Stalag IVB, An Ex-POW Tells His Story, 2004, Authorhouse, ISBN 1-4184-2688-1.

R.H. Jones, A Desert Rat's Tale, The War Diary of Richard H. Jones, [unpublished].

Lucy Mangan, Guardian Weekend, 4/1/2014.

Peter Ogilvie and Newman Robinson, In The Bag, 1975, MacMillan South Africa, ISBN 086954 019 X.

Martin Parr, The Last Resort, 2009, Dewi Lewis Publishing, ISBN 978-1-904587-79-8.

Tony Vercoe, Survival at Stalag IVB, 2006, McFarland and Company, ISBN 0 7864 2404 4.

Visitors Book from the Sandpiper Hotel, New Brighton, 1972 – 1992.